Holiday Ornaments Galore

LEISURE ARTS, INC. • Maumelle, Arkansas

Meet Ursula Michael

Ursula Michael has always loved to sew, paint, and draw. She trained at the Paier College of Art in New Haven, Connecticut. After working several years as a graphic artist, she discovered there was a market for original needlework patterns. Before long, she was selling designs to a variety of publishers and creating her own line of cross stitch kits and patterns.

When she moved from Connecticut to Rhode Island, Ursula began to focus entirely on design work, producing about 200 new designs per year! She filled her workspace with fabric, thread, books, and art materials. In this colorful atmosphere, Ursula currently divides her work hours between her computer, sewing machine, and antique drafting table.

But she also finds time for another important element of life—fun.

"My dog Maverick keeps me company in the studio, which overlooks an ocean bay," she says. "We go for walks and listen to jazz music. And when no one is watching, I sometimes dance to Jimmy Buffet!"

When asked what she likes best about designing needlework, Ursula says, "It's my goal to make the stitcher smile while she works on one of my designs. And I hope that when the same design is finished, it brings joy to whoever sees it."

If you would like to view more of Ursula's joyful artistry and catch up on what she's doing now, visit www.UrsulaMichael.com or join the Let's Stitch Ursula Michael group on Facebook

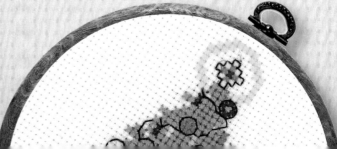

Holiday Ornaments GALORE

Dozens of fun holiday ornaments are just stitches away with the 98 festive images in this book! Brighten the holidays with cheerful elves, jolly Santas, chillin' snowmen, delectable gingerbread men and women, heavenly angels, jaunty reindeer, chirpy birds, adorable bears and more! Trim the tree, tie them to a package, or decorate the house!

GENERAL INSTRUCTIONS

HOW TO READ CHARTS

Each chart is made up of a key and a gridded design on which each square represents a stitch. The symbols in the key tell which floss color to use for each stitch in the chart. The following headings and symbols are given:

⊡✦ **X** — Cross Stitch
    DMC — DMC color number
⊡· **¼ X** — Quarter Stitch
◩ **B'ST** — Backstitch
    ANC. — Anchor color number
    COLOR — The name given to the floss color in that chart

Sometimes the symbol for a Cross Stitch may be partially covered when a Backstitch crosses the square.

HOW TO STITCH

Always work Cross Stitches and Quarter Stitches first and then add the Backstitch. When stitching, bring the threaded needle up at 1 and all odd numbers and down at 2 and all even numbers.

Cross Stitch (X): For horizontal rows, work stitches in two journeys **(Fig. 1)**. For vertical rows, complete each stitch as shown **(Fig. 2)**.

Fig. 1

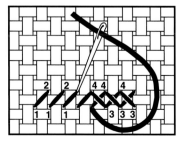

Fig. 2

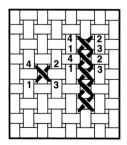

Quarter Stitch (¼X): Come up at 1, and then split the fabric thread to go down at 2 **(Fig. 3)**.

Fig. 3

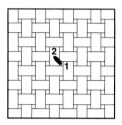

Backstitch (B'ST): For outlines and details, Backstitch should be worked after the design has been completed **(Fig. 4)**.

Fig. 4

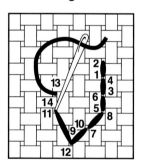

French Knot: Bring the needle up at 1. Wrap the floss once around the needle. Insert the needle at 2, tighten the knot, and pull the needle through the fabric, holding the floss until it must be released (Fig. 5). For a larger knot, use more floss strands and wrap only once.

Fig. 5

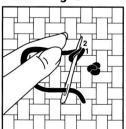

STITCHING TIPS

Preparing Fabric

Being sure to allow plenty of margin, cut the fabric to the desired size and overcast the raw edges. It is better to waste a little fabric than to come up short.

Working with Floss

To ensure smoother stitches, separate the floss strands and realign them before threading the needle. Keep stitching tension consistent. Begin and end the floss by running under several stitches on the back; never tie knots.

Where to Start

The horizontal and vertical center of each charted design is shown by arrows. You may start at any point on the charted design but be sure the design will be centered on the fabric. Locate the center of the fabric by folding it in half, top to bottom and again left to right. On the charted design, count the number of squares (stitches) from the center of the chart to where you wish to start. Then, from the fabric's center, find your starting point by counting out the same number of fabric threads (stitches).

PROJECTS

Each design was stitched on 14 count Aida using 3 strands of floss for Cross Stitch and 1 strand for Backstitch unless otherwise noted. Several of the designs were stitched on 18 count Aida using 2 strands of floss for Cross Stitch and 1 strand for Backstitch unless otherwise noted.
The designs can be made into ornaments, pillows, or added to a frame.

Library of Congress Control Number: 2019933132

Made in U.S.A.

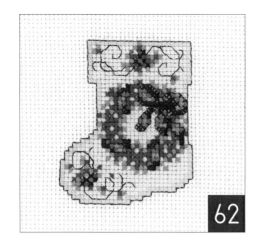

62

51

50

56

63

45

54

46

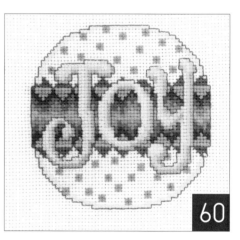

60

52

35

47

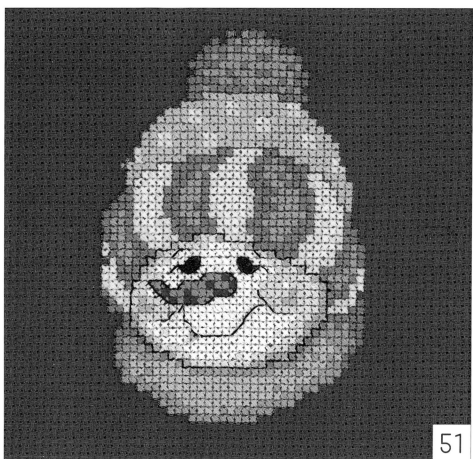

51

48

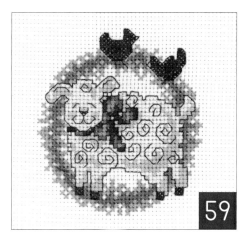

59

58

59

63

60

52

Numbers in corners refer to chart pages.

49

41

42

42

40

49

44

57

58

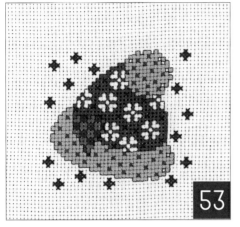

Numbers in corners refer to chart pages.

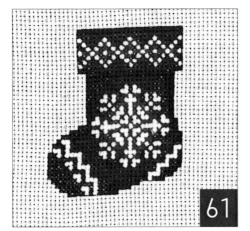

61

64

54

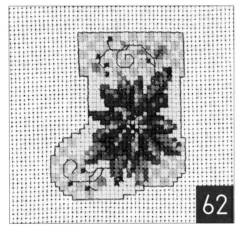

62

23

21

24

20

27

36

41

40

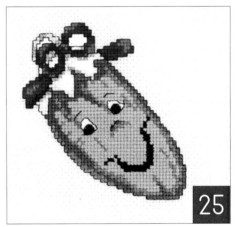

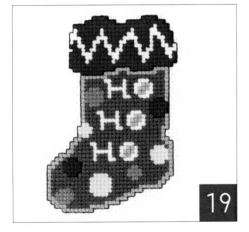

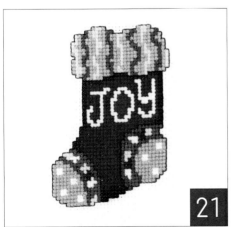

Numbers in corners refer to chart pages.

18

29

26

22

28

16

17

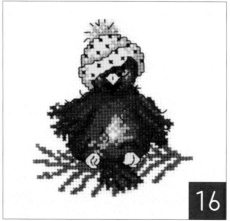

16

24

25

31

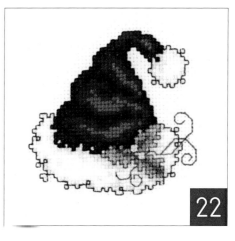

22

39

17

32

30

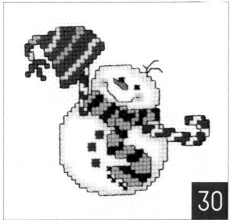

30

39

Numbers in corners refer to chart pages.

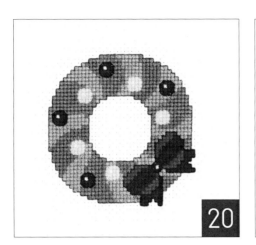 20

 32

 33

 33

 31

 37

 26

 27

 57

 38

 38

 45

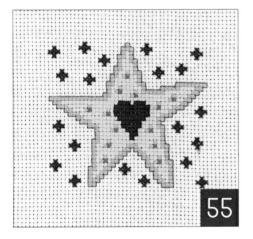 55

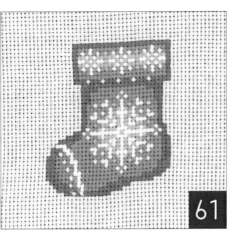 61

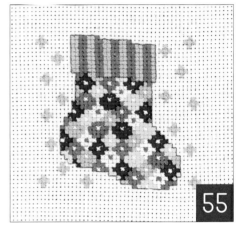 55

 48

 36

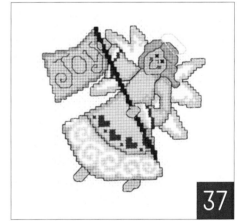 37

 34

 56

 19

Numbers in corners refer to chart pages.

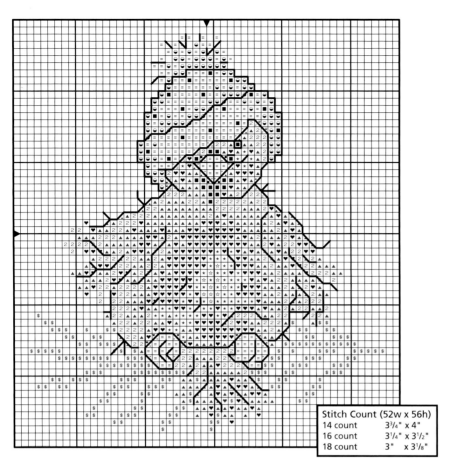

REDBIRD

X	DMC	¼X	B'ST	ANC.	COLOR
☆	blanc			2	white
■	310	◪	◪	403	black
▲	321	◪		9046	red
♥	350	◪		11	coral
★	352			9	peach
$	699			923	dk green
=	726	◪		295	yellow
◡	783	◪		306	gold
2	816	◪		1005	maroon

Design was stitched on an 8" x 8" piece of 14 count white Aida (design size 3³/₄" x 4"). Three strands of floss were used for Cross Stitch and 1 strand for Backstitch. Design was also stitched on a 7" x 7¹/₂" piece of 18 count white Aida (design size 3" x 3¹/₈"). Two strands of floss were used for Cross Stitch and 1 strand for Backstitch.

Shown on page 12.

Stitch Count (52w x 56h)	
14 count	3³/₄" x 4"
16 count	3¹/₄" x 3¹/₂"
18 count	3" x 3¹/₈"

REDBIRD COUPLE

X	DMC	¼X	B'ST	ANC.	COLOR
☆	blanc			2	white
■	310	◪	◪	403	black
m	318			399	grey
▲	321	◪		9046	red
◡	352			9	peach
3	353			6	lt peach
$	699	◪		923	dk green
⁒	701			227	green
+	703	◪		238	lt green
=	726	◪		295	yellow
2	816	◪		1005	maroon

Design was stitched on a 9¹/₂" x 8¹/₂" piece of 14 count white Aida (design size 5¹/₄" x 4¹/₈"). Three strands of floss were used for Cross Stitch and 1 strand for Backstitch.

Shown on page 12.

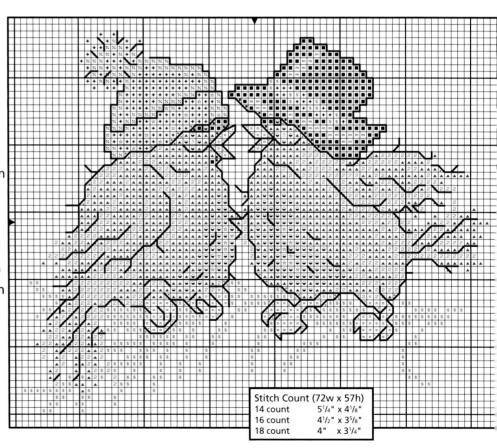

Stitch Count (72w x 57h)	
14 count	5¹/₄" x 4¹/₈"
16 count	4¹/₂" x 3⁵/₈"
18 count	4" x 3¹/₄"

REDBIRD WITH GREEN CAP

X	DMC	¼X	B'ST	ANC.	COLOR
☆	blanc			2	white
■	310	◢	╱	403	black
▲	321	◢		9046	red
◖	351	◢		10	coral
✕	353	◢		6	peach
$	699			923	dk green
╱	701			227	green
+	703	◢		238	lt green
C	726	◢		295	yellow
♥	816			1005	maroon

Design was stitched on an 8" x 8" piece of 14 count white Aida (design size 3⅝" x 3¾"). Three strands of floss were used for Cross Stitch and 1 strand for Backstitch. Design was also stitched on a 7" x 7" piece of 18 count white Aida (design size 2⅞" x 2⅞"). Two strands of floss were used for Cross Stitch and 1 strand for Backstitch.

Shown on page 12.

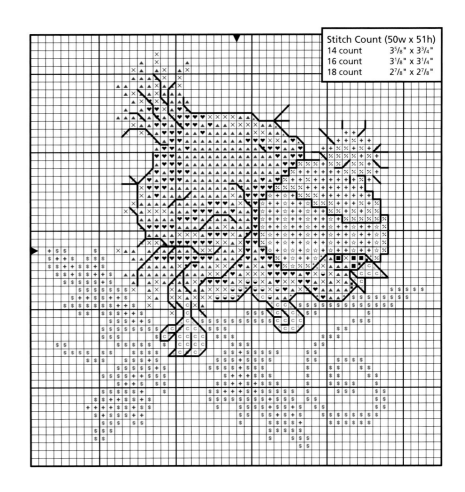

Stitch Count (50w x 51h)
14 count	3⅝" x 3¾"
16 count	3⅛" x 3¼"
18 count	2⅞" x 2⅞"

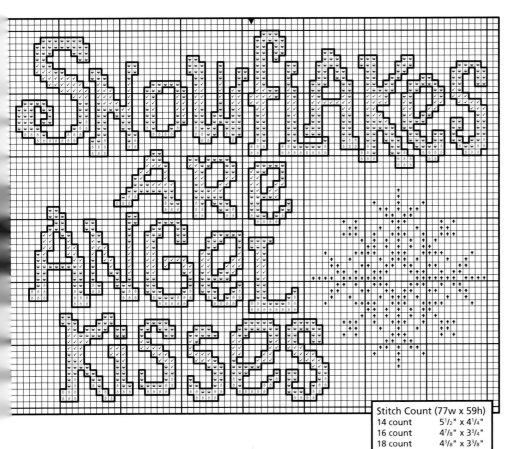

ANGEL KISSES

X	DMC	B'ST	ANC.	COLOR
8	797	╱	132	dk blue
◡	799		136	blue
✓	800		144	lt blue
♠	995		410	turquoise

Design was stitched on a 9½" x 8½" piece of 14 count white Aida (design size 5½" x 4¼"). Three strands of floss were used for Cross Stitch and 1 strand for Backstitch.

Shown on page 13.

Stitch Count (77w x 59h)
14 count	5½" x 4¼"
16 count	4⅞" x 3¾"
18 count	4⅜" x 3⅜"

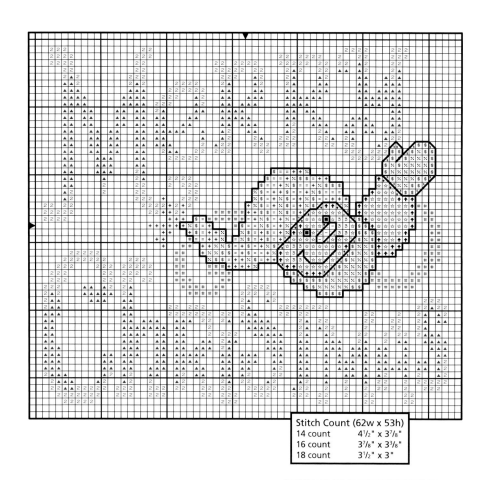

MERRY CHRISTMAS

X	DMC	1/4X	B'ST	ANC.	COLOR
☆	blanc	◿		2	white
■	310		╱	403	black
▲	321			9046	red
3	353			6	peach
$	699	◿$		923	dk green
%	701			227	green
+	703	◿+		238	lt green
=	726	◿=		295	yellow
↑	762	◿↑		234	lt grey
#	809			130	blue
2	816			1005	maroon
−	970	◿		316	orange

Design was stitched on an 8¹/₂" x 8" piece of 14 count white Aida (design size 4¹/₂" x 3⁷/₈"). Three strands of floss were used for Cross Stitch and 1 strand for Backstitch.

Shown on page 11.

Stitch Count (62w x 53h)
14 count   4¹/₂" x 3⁷/₈"
16 count   3⁷/₈" x 3³/₈"
18 count   3¹/₂" x 3"

NOEL

X	DMC	B'ST	ANC.	COLOR
▲	321		9046	red
$	699		923	dk green
%	701	╱	227	green
+	703		238	lt green

Design was stitched on an 8" x 8" piece of 14 count white Aida (design size 3⁷/₈" x 4"). Three strands of floss were used for Cross Stitch and 1 strand for Backstitch.

Shown on page 12.

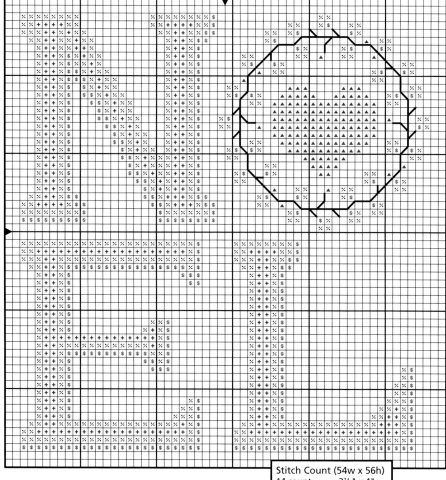

Stitch Count (54w x 56h)
14 count   3⁷/₈" x 4"
16 count   3³/₈" x 3¹/₂"
18 count   3"   x 3¹/₈"

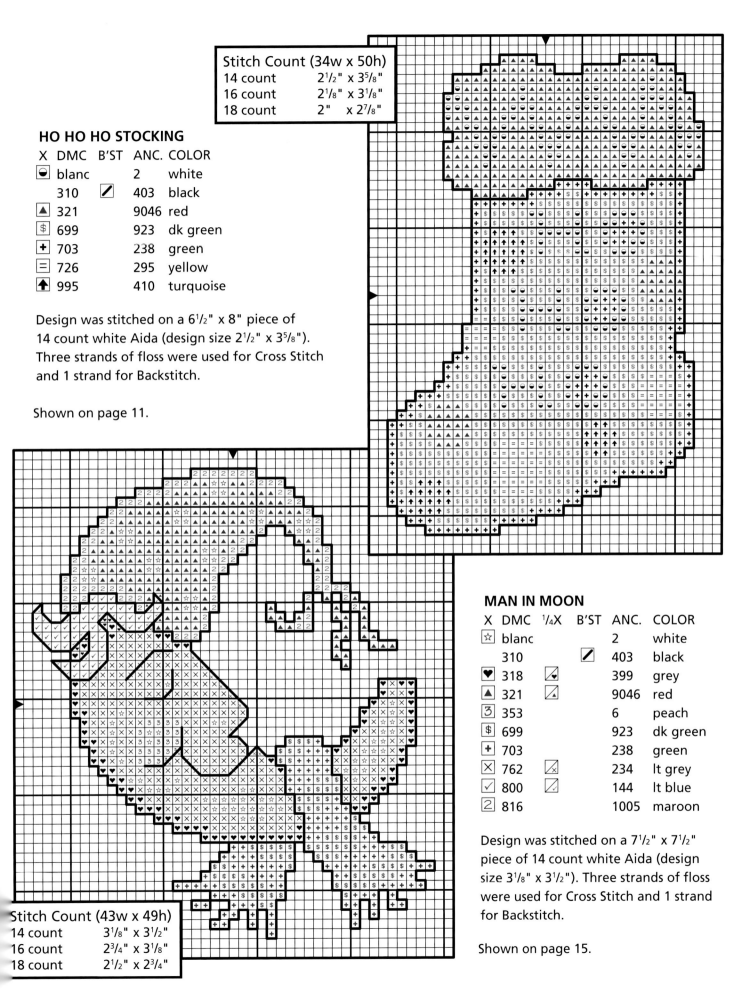

Stitch Count (34w x 50h)

14 count	2½"	x 3⅝"
16 count	2⅛"	x 3⅛"
18 count	2"	x 2⅞"

HO HO HO STOCKING

X	DMC	B'ST	ANC.	COLOR
⊖	blanc		2	white
	310	✓	403	black
▲	321		9046	red
$	699		923	dk green
+	703		238	green
=	726		295	yellow
⬆	995		410	turquoise

Design was stitched on a 6½" x 8" piece of 14 count white Aida (design size 2½" x 3⅝"). Three strands of floss were used for Cross Stitch and 1 strand for Backstitch.

Shown on page 11.

Stitch Count (43w x 49h)

14 count	3⅛"	x 3½"
16 count	2¾"	x 3⅛"
18 count	2½"	x 2¾"

MAN IN MOON

X	DMC	¼X	B'ST	ANC.	COLOR
☆	blanc			2	white
	310		✓	403	black
♥	318	◢		399	grey
▲	321	◿		9046	red
3	353			6	peach
$	699			923	dk green
+	703			238	green
✕	762	◳		234	lt grey
✓	800	◿		144	lt blue
2	816			1005	maroon

Design was stitched on a 7½" x 7½" piece of 14 count white Aida (design size 3⅛" x 3½"). Three strands of floss were used for Cross Stitch and 1 strand for Backstitch.

Shown on page 15.

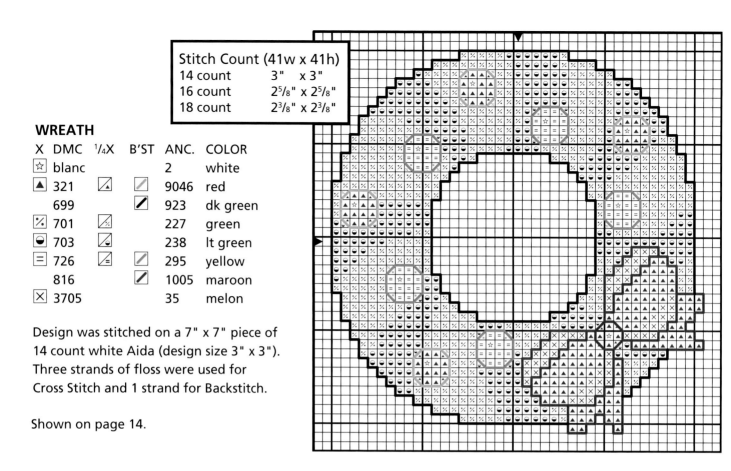

Stitch Count (41w x 41h)

14 count	3" x 3"
16 count	2⅝" x 2⅝"
18 count	2⅜" x 2⅜"

WREATH

X	DMC	¼X	B'ST	ANC.	COLOR
☆	blanc			2	white
▲	321	◩	◪	9046	red
	699		◪	923	dk green
◪	701	◩		227	green
◖	703	◪		238	lt green
=	726	◩	◪	295	yellow
	816		◪	1005	maroon
☒	3705			35	melon

Design was stitched on a 7" x 7" piece of 14 count white Aida (design size 3" x 3"). Three strands of floss were used for Cross Stitch and 1 strand for Backstitch.

Shown on page 14.

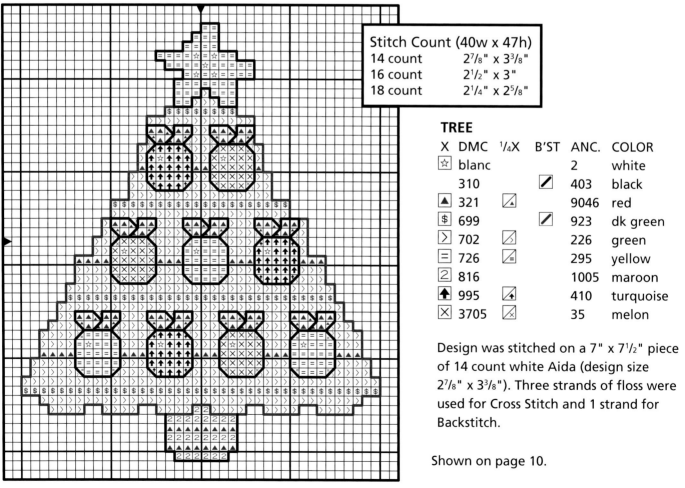

Stitch Count (40w x 47h)

14 count	2⅞" x 3⅜"
16 count	2½" x 3"
18 count	2¼" x 2⅝"

TREE

X	DMC	¼X	B'ST	ANC.	COLOR
☆	blanc			2	white
	310		◪	403	black
▲	321	◩		9046	red
$	699		◪	923	dk green
❯	702	◩		226	green
=	726	◩		295	yellow
☑	816			1005	maroon
⬆	995	◪		410	turquoise
☒	3705	◪		35	melon

Design was stitched on a 7" x 7½" piece of 14 count white Aida (design size 2⅞" x 3⅜"). Three strands of floss were used for Cross Stitch and 1 strand for Backstitch.

Shown on page 10.

JOY STOCKING

X	DMC	B'ST	ANC.	COLOR
☆	blanc		2	white
	310	✎	403	black
▲	321		9046	red
$	699		923	dk green
+	703		238	green
=	726		295	yellow
✖	797		132	dk blue
♥	816		1005	dk red

Design was stitched on a 6¹⁄₂" x 8" piece of 14 count white Aida (design size 2¹⁄₂" x 3⁵⁄₈"). Three strands of floss were used for Cross Stitch and 1 strand for Backstitch.

Shown on page 11.

Stitch Count (34w x 50h)		
14 count	2¹⁄₂"	x 3⁵⁄₈"
16 count	2¹⁄₈"	x 3¹⁄₈"
18 count	2"	x 2⁷⁄₈"

Stitch Count (35w x 58h)		
14 count	2¹⁄₂"	x 4¹⁄₄"
16 count	2¹⁄₄"	x 3⁵⁄₈"
18 count	2"	x 3¹⁄₄"

BLUE CAP

X	DMC	B'ST	ANC.	COLOR
☆	blanc		2	white
♥	415		398	lt grey
+	703		238	green
ß	797	✎	132	dk blue
◆	799		136	lt blue

Design was stitched on a 6¹⁄₂" x 8¹⁄₂" piece of 14 count white Aida (design size 2¹⁄₂" x 4¹⁄₄"). Three strands of floss were used for Cross Stitch and 1 strand for Backstitch.

Shown on page 10.

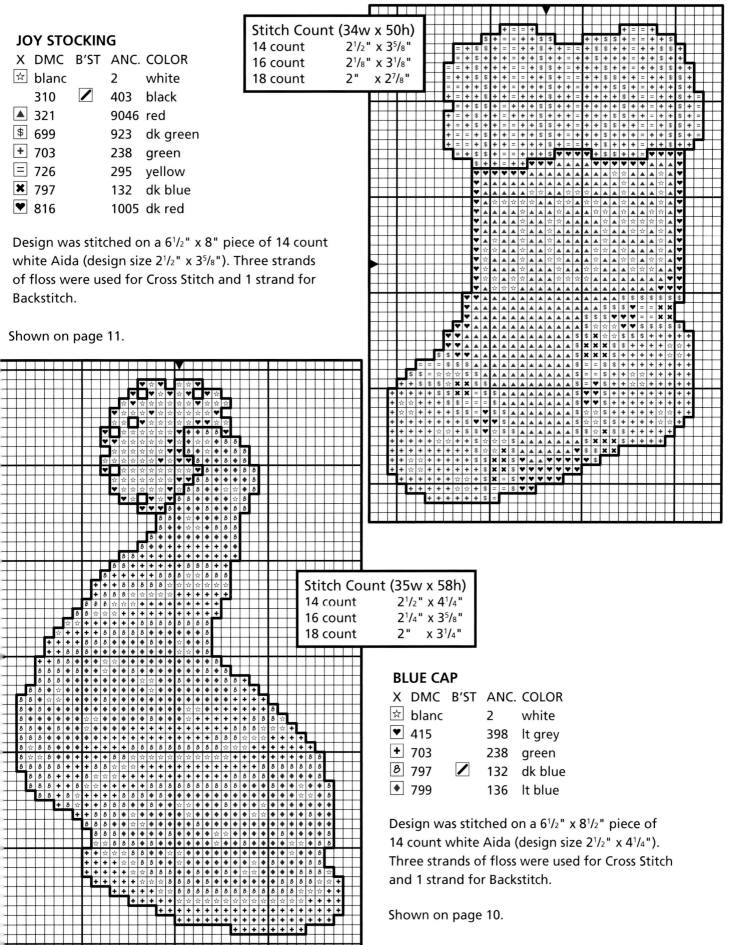

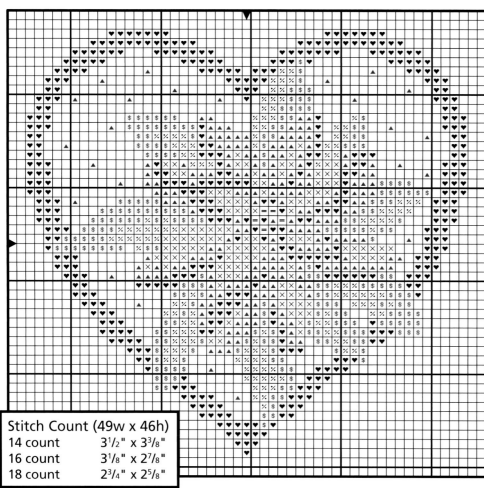

POINSETTIA HEART

X	DMC	ANC.	COLOR
▲	321	9046	red
$	699	923	dk green
‰	702	226	green
=	726	295	yellow
♥	816	1005	maroon
✕	3705	35	melon

Design was stitched on a 7$\frac{1}{2}$" x 7$\frac{1}{2}$" piece of 14 count white Aida (design size 3$\frac{1}{2}$" x 3$\frac{3}{8}$"). Three strands of floss were used for Cross Stitch.

Shown on page 12.

Stitch Count (49w x 46h)
14 count	3$\frac{1}{2}$" x 3$\frac{3}{8}$"
16 count	3$\frac{1}{8}$" x 2$\frac{7}{8}$"
18 count	2$\frac{3}{4}$" x 2$\frac{5}{8}$"

SANTA HAT

X	DMC	B'ST	ANC.	COLOR
☆	blanc		2	white
▲	321		9046	red
$	699	✏	923	dk green
‰	701		227	green
+	703		238	lt green
=	726		295	yellow
◓	762		234	lt grey
♥	816	✏	1005	maroon
✕	3705		35	melon

Design was stitched on a 7$\frac{1}{2}$" x 7$\frac{1}{2}$" piece of 14 count white Aida (design size 3$\frac{3}{8}$" x 3$\frac{1}{8}$"). Three strands of floss were used for Cross Stitch and 1 strand for Backstitch. Design was also stitched on a 7" x 6$\frac{1}{2}$" piece of 18 count white Aida (design size 2$\frac{5}{8}$" x 2$\frac{1}{2}$"). Two strands of floss were used for Cross Stitch and 1 strand for Backstitch.

Shown on page 13.

Stitch Count (46w x 43h)
14 count	3$\frac{3}{8}$" x 3$\frac{1}{8}$"
16 count	2$\frac{7}{8}$" x 2$\frac{3}{4}$"
18 count	2$\frac{5}{8}$" x 2$\frac{1}{2}$"

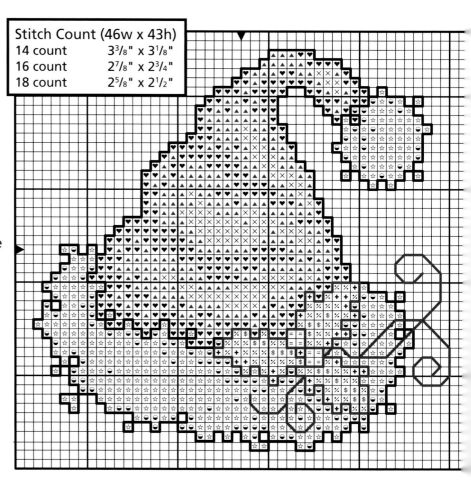

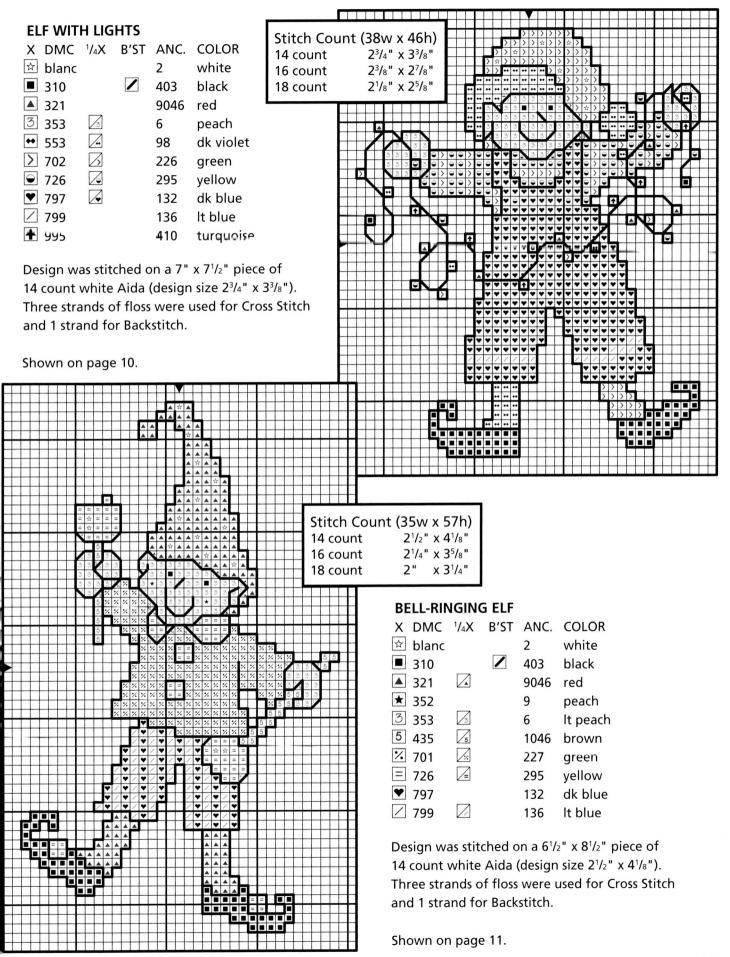

ELF WITH LIGHTS

X	DMC	1/4X	B'ST	ANC.	COLOR
☆	blanc			2	white
■	310		╱	403	black
▲	321			9046	red
3	353	3		6	peach
✤	553	✤		98	dk violet
>	702	>		226	green
◑	726	◑		295	yellow
♥	797	♥		132	dk blue
╱	799			136	lt blue
♠	995			410	turquoise

Design was stitched on a 7" x 7½" piece of 14 count white Aida (design size 2¾" x 3⅜"). Three strands of floss were used for Cross Stitch and 1 strand for Backstitch.

Shown on page 10.

Stitch Count (38w x 46h)	
14 count	2¾" x 3⅜"
16 count	2⅜" x 2⅞"
18 count	2⅛" x 2⅝"

Stitch Count (35w x 57h)	
14 count	2½" x 4⅛"
16 count	2¼" x 3⅝"
18 count	2" x 3¼"

BELL-RINGING ELF

X	DMC	1/4X	B'ST	ANC.	COLOR
☆	blanc			2	white
■	310		╱	403	black
▲	321	▲		9046	red
★	352			9	peach
3	353	3		6	lt peach
5	435	5		1046	brown
╱	701	╱		227	green
=	726	=		295	yellow
♥	797			132	dk blue
╱	799		╱	136	lt blue

Design was stitched on a 6½" x 8½" piece of 14 count white Aida (design size 2½" x 4⅛"). Three strands of floss were used for Cross Stitch and 1 strand for Backstitch.

Shown on page 11.

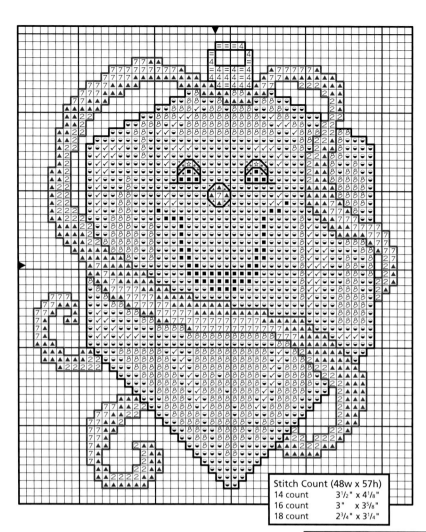

BLUE ORNAMENT

X	DMC	¼X	B'ST	ANC.	COLOR
☆	blanc	◹	☆	2	white
■	310	◪	╱	403	black
▲	321	◹		9046	red
=	726			295	lt yellow
8	797			132	dk blue
◓	799	◹		136	blue
✓	800			144	lt blue
2	816		╱	1005	maroon
7	3705			35	lt red
4	3852			306	gold

Design was stitched on a 7½" x 8½" piece of 14 count white Aida (design size 3½" x 4⅛"). Three strands of floss were used for Cross Stitch and 1 strand for Backstitch.

Shown on page 10.

Stitch Count (48w x 57h)
14 count	3½" x 4⅛"
16 count	3" x 3⅝"
18 count	2¾" x 3¼"

RED ORNAMENT

X	DMC	¼X	B'ST	ANC.	COLOR
☆	blanc	◹		2	white
■	310	◪	╱	403	black
m	318			399	grey
▲	321	◹		9046	red
$	699	◹	╱	923	dk green
%	701			227	green
+	703			238	lt green
=	726			295	yellow
◓	762			234	lt grey
2	816			1005	maroon
7	3705			35	lt red
4	3852			306	gold

Design was stitched on an 8" x 8" piece of 14 count white Aida (design size 3¾" x 3¾"). Three strands of floss were used for Cross Stitch and 1 strand for Backstitch.

Shown on page 12.

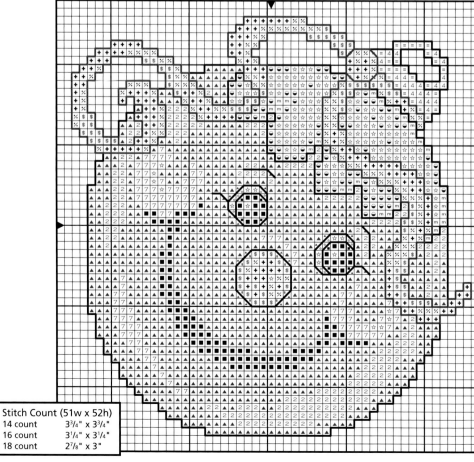

Stitch Count (51w x 52h)
14 count	3¾" x 3¾"
16 count	3¼" x 3¼"
18 count	2⅞" x 3"

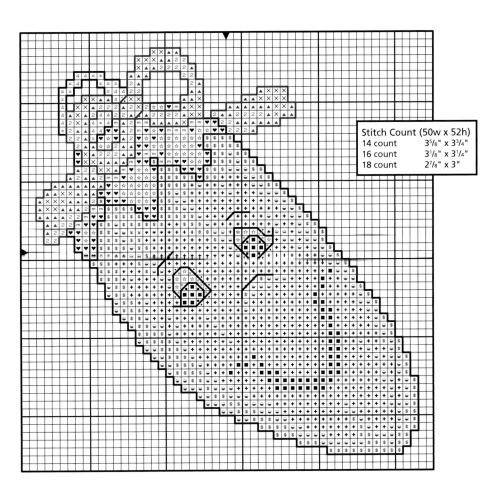

Stitch Count (50w x 52h)
14 count	3⁵/₈"	x 3³/₄"
16 count	3¹/₈"	x 3¹/₄"
18 count	2⁷/₈"	x 3"

GREEN ORNAMENT

X	DMC	¹/₄X	B'ST	ANC.	COLOR
☆	blanc	⟋☆		2	white
■	310	⟋■	⟋	403	black
m	318			399	grey
▲	321	⟋		9046	red
$	699			923	dk green
◡	701	⟋◡		227	green
+	703	⟋+		238	lt green
=	726			295	yellow
♥	762			234	lt grey
2	816		⟋	1005	maroon
✕	3705			35	melon
4	3852	⟋4		306	gold

Design was stitched on an 8" x 8" piece of 14 count white Aida (design size 3⁵/₈" x 3³/₄"). Three strands of floss were used for Cross Stitch and 1 strand for Backstitch.

Shown on page 11.

REINDEER

X	DMC	¹/₄X	B'ST	ANC.	COLOR
☆	blanc	⟋☆		2	white
■	310	⟋■	⟋	403	black
▲	321	⟋		9046	red
3	351			10	coral
4	433			358	brown
◡	436	⟋◡		1045	tan
◆	554			96	violet
$	699	⟋$	⟋	923	dk green
+	703			238	green
=	726	⟋=		295	yellow
@	738			361	lt tan
	816		⟋	1005	maroon
♥	927			848	grey green
⬆	995			410	turquoise

Design was stitched on an 8"x 8¹/₂" piece of 14 count white Aida (design size 3³/₄" x 4¹/₈"). Three strands of floss were used for Cross Stitch and 1 strand for Backstitch.

Shown on page 13.

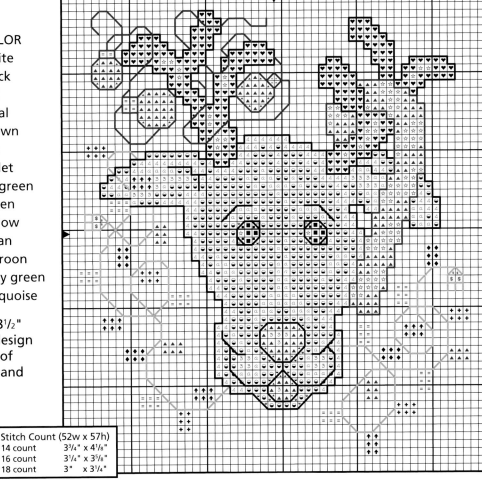

Stitch Count (52w x 57h)
14 count	3³/₄"	x 4¹/₈"
16 count	3¹/₄"	x 3⁵/₈"
18 count	3"	x 3¹/₄"

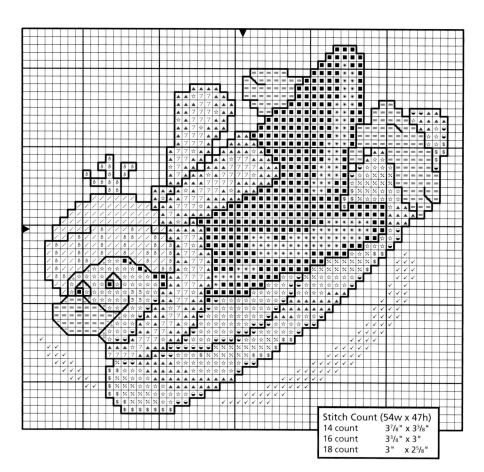

SLEDDING PENGUIN

X	DMC	1/4X	B'ST	ANC.	COLOR
☆	blanc			2	white
■	310		/	403	black
✳	317			400	grey
▲	321			9046	red
3	353			6	peach
⬮	415			398	lt grey
$	699			923	dk green
%	701			227	green
=	726			295	yellow
8	797			132	dk blue
/	799			136	blue
✓	800			144	lt blue
7	3705			35	lt red

Design was stitched on an 8" x 7½" piece of 14 count white Aida (design size 3⅞" x 3⅜"). Three strands of floss were used for Cross Stitch and 1 strand for Backstitch.

Shown on page 12.

Stitch Count (54w x 47h)	
14 count	3⅞" x 3⅜"
16 count	3⅜" x 3"
18 count	3" x 2⅝"

PENGUIN WITH CANDY CANE

X	DMC	1/4X	B'ST	ANC.	COLOR
☆	blanc			2	white
■	310		/	403	black
✳	317			400	grey
▲	321			9046	red
◇	415			398	lt grey
$	699			923	dk green
⬮	702			226	green
=	726			295	yellow
2	816			1005	maroon
✕	3705			35	melon

Design was stitched on a 7½" x 8½" piece of 14 count white Aida (design size 3⅛" x 4¼"). Three strands of floss were used for Cross Stitch and 1 strand for Backstitch.

Shown on page 14.

Stitch Count (44w x 58h)	
14 count	3⅛" x 4¼"
16 count	2¾" x 3⅝"
18 count	2½" x 3¼"

SKIING PENGUIN

X	DMC	¼X	B'ST	ANC.	COLOR
☆	blanc	◿		2	white
■	310	◩	◢	403	black
m	318			399	grey
▲	321	◿		9046	red
◇	415			398	lt grey
◆	554			96	violet
+	703			238	green
=	726	◿		295	yellow
8	797			132	dk blue
√	800			144	lt blue
2	816	◿		1005	maroon
✕	3705			35	melon

Design was stitched on an 8" x 8½" piece of 14 count white Aida (design size 4" x 3⅛"). Three strands of floss were used for Cross Stitch and 1 strand for Backstitch.

Shown on page 14.

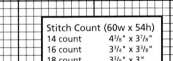

Stitch Count (55w x 57h)
14 count	4"	x 4⅛"
16 count	3½"	x 3⅝"
18 count	3⅛"	x 3¼"

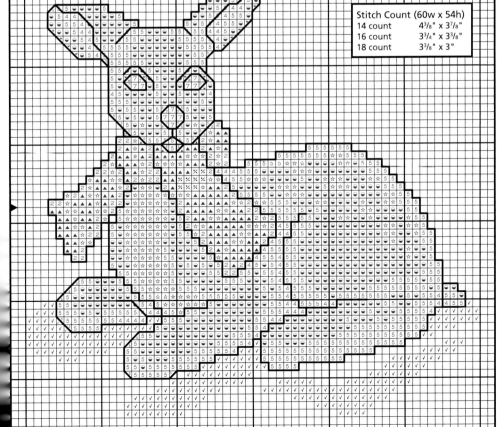

Stitch Count (60w x 54h)
14 count	4⅜"	x 3⅞"
16 count	3¾"	x 3⅜"
18 count	3⅜"	x 3"

BABY DEER

X	DMC	¼X	B'ST	ANC.	COLOR
☆	blanc	◿		2	white
▲	321	◿		9046	red
4	433			358	dk brown
5	435	◿		1046	brown
◓	437	◿		362	dk tan
⊘	701			227	green
√	800	◿		144	lt blue
2	816	◿		1005	maroon
7	3371	◿	◢	382	black brown

Design was stitched on an 8½" x 8" piece of 14 count white Aida (design size 4⅜" x 3⅞"). Three strands of floss were used for Cross Stitch and 1 strand for Backstitch.

Shown on page 10.

27

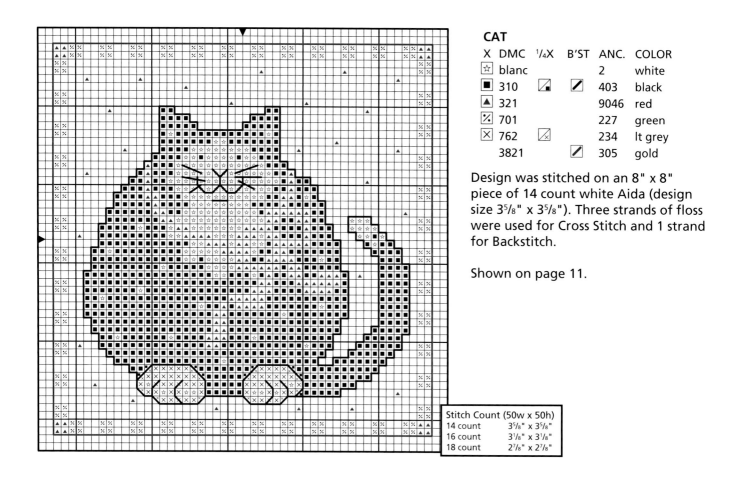

CAT

X	DMC	¼X	B'ST	ANC.	COLOR
☆	blanc			2	white
■	310		/	403	black
▲	321			9046	red
%	701			227	green
X	762			234	lt grey
	3821		/	305	gold

Design was stitched on an 8" x 8" piece of 14 count white Aida (design size 3⅝" x 3⅝"). Three strands of floss were used for Cross Stitch and 1 strand for Backstitch.

Shown on page 11.

Stitch Count (50w x 50h)
14 count   3⅝" x 3⅝"
16 count   3⅛" x 3⅛"
18 count   2⅞" x 2⅞"

PUPPY

X	DMC	¼X	B'ST	ANC.	COLOR
☆	blanc			2	white
♥	318			399	grey
▲	321			9046	red
☻	436			1045	tan
%	701			227	green
+	703			238	lt green
@	738			361	lt tan
X	762			234	lt grey
7	3371		/	382	black brown
△	3705			35	melon

Design was stitched on an 8½" x 8" piece of 14 count white Aida (design size 4¼" x 4"). Three strands of floss were used for Cross Stitch and 1 strand for Backstitch.

Shown on page 12.

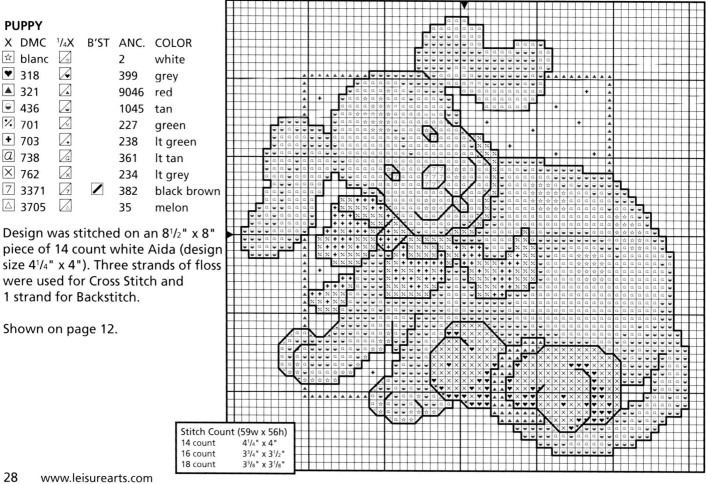

Stitch Count (59w x 56h)
14 count   4¼" x 4"
16 count   3¾" x 3½"
18 count   3⅜" x 3⅛"

PEACE BEARS

X	DMC	¼X	B'ST	ANC.	COLOR
☆	blanc			2	white
■	310		/	403	black
◆	318			399	grey
$	699		/	923	dk green
+	703			238	green
↑	762			234	lt grey

Design was stitched on an 8" x 8" piece of 14 count white Aida (design size 4" x 3³/₄"). Three strands of floss were used for Cross Stitch and 1 strand for Backstitch.

Shown on page 12.

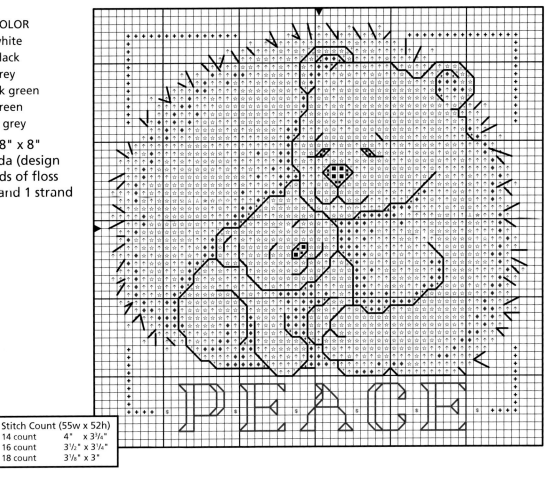

Stitch Count (55w x 52h)
14 count   4"   x 3³/₄"
16 count   3¹/₂" x 3¹/₄"
18 count   3¹/₈" x 3"

GINGERBREAD COUPLE

X	DMC	¼X	B'ST	ANC.	COLOR
☆	blanc			2	white
■	310		/	403	black
▲	321		/	9046	red
◆	415			398	lt grey
5	435			1046	brown
⁒	701			227	green
+	703			238	lt green
=	726			295	yellow
ⓐ	738			361	lt tan
/	799			136	lt blue
H	801			359	dk brown
2	816			1005	maroon
✕	3705			35	melon

Design was stitched on an 8¹/₂" x 8" piece of 14 count white Aida (design size 4¹/₄" x 3⁷/₈"). Three strands of floss were used for Cross Stitch and 1 strand for Backstitch.

Shown on page 11.

Stitch Count (58w x 53h)
14 count   4¹/₄" x 3⁷/₈"
16 count   3⁵/₈" x 3³/₈"
18 count   3¹/₄" x 3"

29

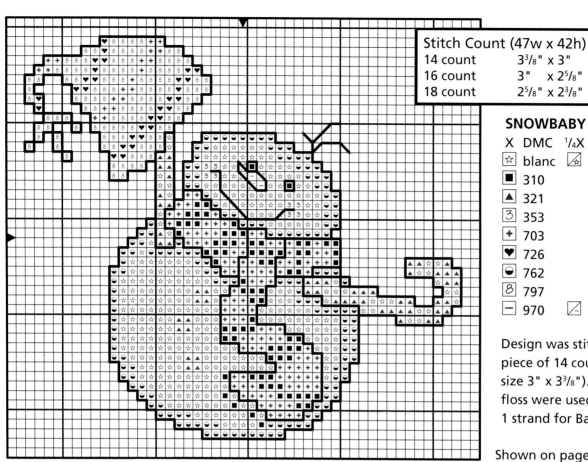

Stitch Count (47w x 42h)
14 count	3³/₈"	x 3"
16 count	3"	x 2⁵/₈"
18 count	2⁵/₈"	x 2³/₈"

SNOWBABY WITH BLUE CAP

X	DMC	¼X	B'ST	ANC.	COLOR
☆	blanc	◩		2	white
■	310		◹	403	black
▲	321			9046	red
₃	353			6	peach
+	703			238	green
♥	726			295	yellow
◓	762			234	lt grey
၆	797			132	blue
−	970	◪		316	orange

Design was stitched on a 7¹/₂" x 7" piece of 14 count white Aida (design size 3" x 3³/₈"). Three strands of floss were used for Cross Stitch and 1 strand for Backstitch.

Shown on page 13.

SNOWBABY

X	DMC	¼X	B'ST	ANC.	COLOR
☆	blanc	◩		2	white
■	310		◹	403	black
▲	321			9046	red
₃	353			6	peach
⁒	701			227	green
◓	762			234	lt grey
၆	797			132	blue
−	970	◪		316	orange
↑	995			410	turquoise

Design was stitched on a 7" x 7¹/₂" piece of 14 count white Aida (design size 3" x 3³/₈"). Three strands of floss were used for Cross Stitch and 1 strand for Backstitch.

Shown on page 13.

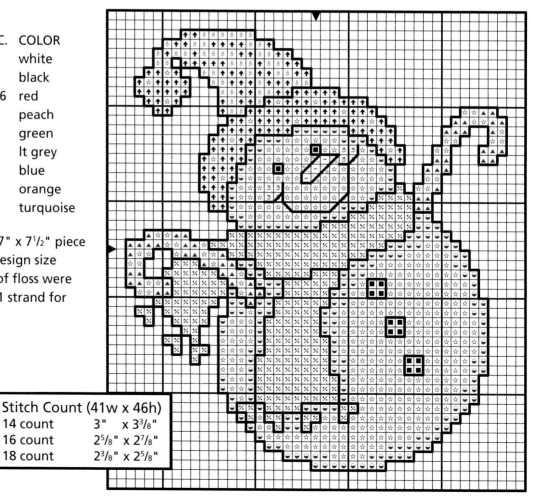

Stitch Count (41w x 46h)
14 count	3"	x 3³/₈"
16 count	2⁵/₈"	x 2⁷/₈"
18 count	2³/₈"	x 2⁵/₈"

ROLYPOLY SANTA

X	DMC	¼X	B'ST	ANC.	COLOR
☆	blanc			2	white
■	310		╱	403	black
▲	321			9046	red
★	352			9	peach
③	353			6	lt peach
+	703			238	green
=	726			295	yellow
◖	762			234	lt grey
②	816			1005	maroon

Design was stitched on a 7½" x 7½" piece of 14 count white Aida (design size 3⅛" x 3½"). Three strands of floss were used for Cross Stitch and 1 strand for Backstitch. Design was also stitched on a 6½" x 7" piece of 18 count white Aida (design size 2½" x 2¾"). Two strands of floss were used for Cross Stitch and 1 strand for Backstitch.

Shown on page 13.

Stitch Count (43w x 49h)	
14 count	3⅛" x 3½"
16 count	2¾" x 3⅛"
18 count	2½" x 2¾"

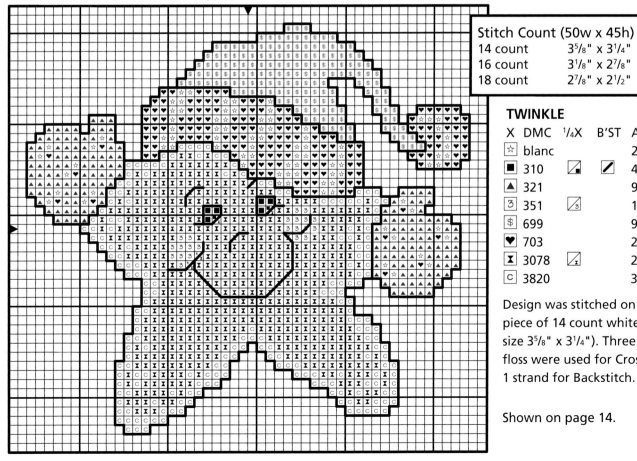

Stitch Count (50w x 45h)	
14 count	3⅝" x 3¼"
16 count	3⅛" x 2⅞"
18 count	2⅞" x 2½"

TWINKLE

X	DMC	¼X	B'ST	ANC.	COLOR
☆	blanc			2	white
■	310	◢	╱	403	black
▲	321			9046	red
③	351			10	coral
$	699			923	green
♥	703			238	lt green
✖	3078	◢		292	lt yellow
C	3820			306	lt gold

Design was stitched on an 8" x 7½" piece of 14 count white Aida (design size 3⅝" x 3¼"). Three strands of floss were used for Cross Stitch and 1 strand for Backstitch.

Shown on page 14.

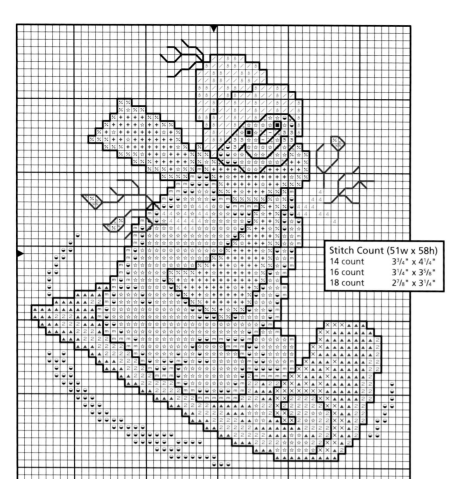

SLEDDING SNOWMAN

X	DMC	¼X	B'ST	ANC.	COLOR
☆	blanc			2	white
■	310		╱	403	black
m	318			399	grey
▲	321			9046	red
3	353			6	peach
4	433		╱	358	brown
⁒	701	⧄		227	green
+	703	⧄		238	lt green
◖	762	⧄		234	lt grey
8	797			132	blue
╱	799	⧄		136	lt blue
2	816			1005	maroon
−	970	⧄		316	orange
✕	3705			35	melon

Design was stitched on an 8" x 8½" piece of 14 count white Aida (design size 3¾" x 4¼"). Three strands of floss were used for Cross Stitch and 1 strand for Backstitch.

Shown on page 13.

SKIING SNOWMAN

X	DMC	¼X	B'ST	ANC.	COLOR
☆	blanc	⧄		2	white
■	310		╱	403	black
m	318			399	grey
▲	321			9046	red
3	353			6	peach
4	433		╱	358	brown
⁒	701	⧄		227	green
+	703			238	lt green
=	726			295	yellow
◖	762	⧄		234	lt grey
♥	797	⧄		132	blue
╱	799			136	lt blue
2	816	⧄		1005	maroon
−	970	⧄		316	orange
⬆	995			410	turquoise

Design was stitched on a 7½" x 8" piece of 14 count white Aida (design size 3½" x 4"). Three strands of floss were used for Cross Stitch and 1 strand for Backstitch. Design was also stitched on a 7" x 7½" piece of 18 count white Aida (design size 2¾" x 3⅛"). Two strands of floss were used for Cross Stitch and 1 strand for Backstitch.

Shown on page 14.

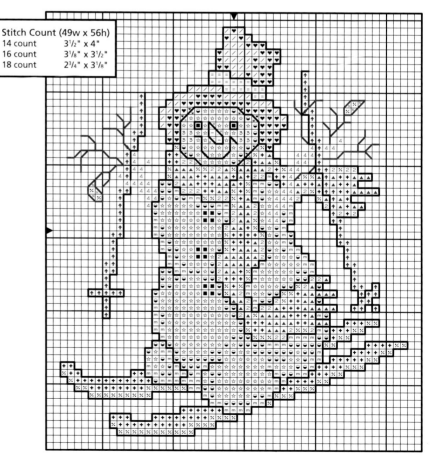

Stitch Count (49w x 56h)
14 count   3½" x 4"
16 count   3⅛" x 3½"
18 count   2¾" x 3⅛"

SKATING SNOWMAN

X	DMC	¼X	B'ST	ANC.	COLOR
☆	blanc	◩		2	white
■	310		╱	403	black
m	318			399	grey
3	353			6	peach
♥	433		╱	358	brown
◆	554	◪		96	violet
⅋	701			227	green
+	703	◪		238	lt green
◡	762	◪		234	lt grey
✖	797			132	blue
−	970	◪		316	orange

Design was stitched on a 7½" x 7½" piece of 14 count white Aida (design size 3⅜" x 3¼"). Three strands of floss were used for Cross Stitch and 1 strand for Backstitch.

Shown on page 14.

Stitch Count (46w x 45h)		
14 count	3⅜" x 3¼"	
16 count	2⅞" x 2⅞"	
18 count	2⅝" x 2½"	

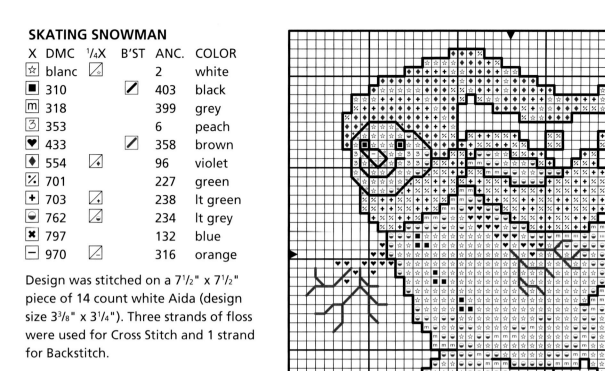

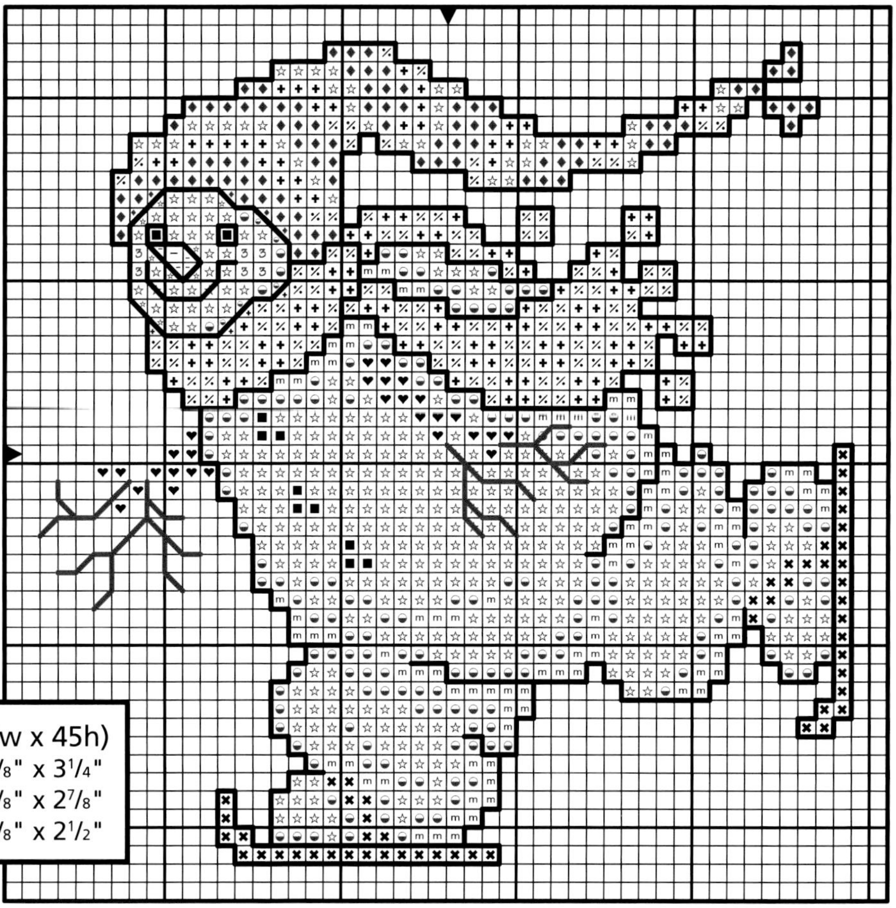

Stitch Count (48w x 44h)		
14 count	3½" x 3¼"	
16 count	3" x 2¾"	
18 count	2¾" x 2½"	

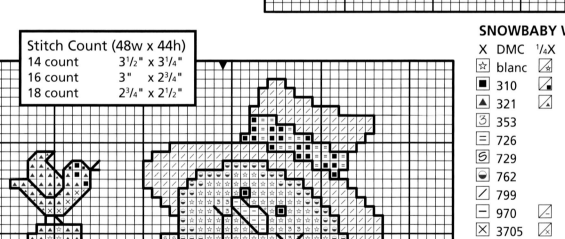

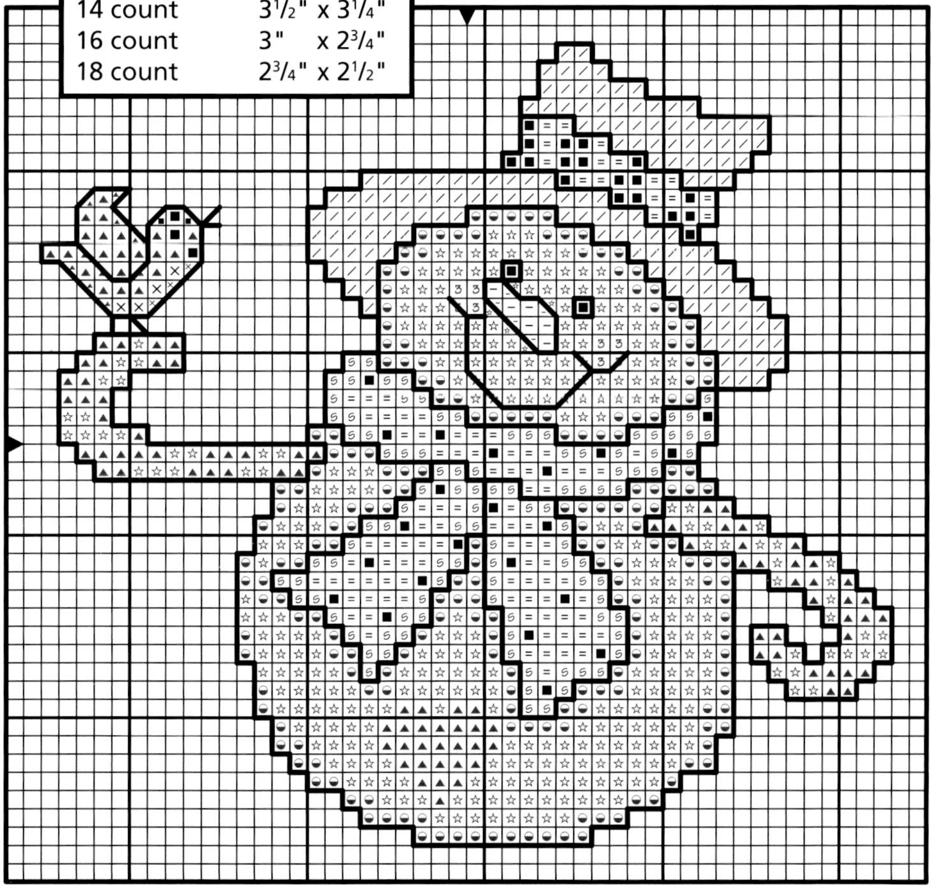

SNOWBABY WITH REDBIRD

X	DMC	¼X	B'ST	ANC.	COLOR
☆	blanc	◩		2	white
■	310	◪	╱	403	black
▲	321	◪		9046	red
3	353			6	peach
=	726			295	yellow
S	729			890	gold
◡	762			234	lt grey
╱	799			136	blue
−	970	◪		316	orange
✕	3705	◪		35	melon

Design was stitched on a 7½" x 7½" piece of 14 count white Aida (design size 3½" x 3¼"). Three strands of floss were used for Cross Stitch and 1 strand for Backstitch. Design was also stitched on a 7" x 6½" piece of 18 count white Aida (design size 2¾" x 2½"). Two strands of floss were used for Cross Stitch and 1 strand for Backstitch.

Shown on page 14.

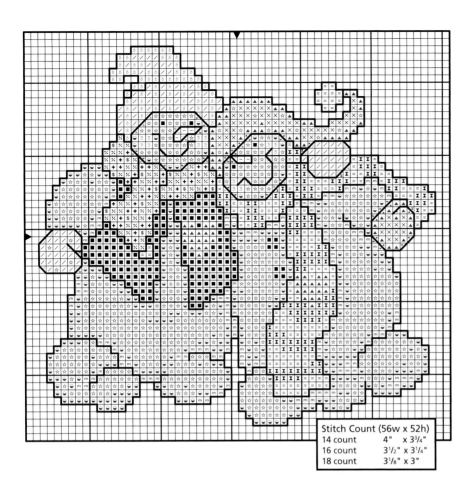

SNOW COUPLE

X	DMC	¼X	B'ST	ANC.	COLOR
☆	blanc	⊠		2	white
■	310		◢	403	black
m	318	▨		399	grey
▲	321	◿		9046	red
③	353			6	peach
$	699			923	dk green
%	701	◿		227	green
+	703			238	lt green
=	726	◿		295	yellow
⌣	762	◿		234	lt grey
8	797	◿		132	blue
/	799	◿		136	lt blue
−	970	◿		316	orange
⌶	3078	◿		292	lt yellow
⊠	3705			35	melon

Design was stitched on an 8" x 8" piece of 14 count white Aida (design size 4" x 3¾"). Three strands of floss were used for Cross Stitch and 1 strand for Backstitch.

Shown on page 15.

Stitch Count (56w x 52h)
14 count	4"	x 3¾"
16 count	3½"	x 3¼"
18 count	3⅛"	x 3"

JINGLE BELLS

X	DMC	¼X	B'ST	ANC.	COLOR
☆	blanc			2	white
■	310		◢	403	black
▲	321			9046	red
%	701	◿		227	green
+	703	◿		238	lt green
♥	726	◿		295	yellow
	797		◢	132	dk blue
⌣	799	◿		136	lt blue
#	809			130	blue
④	3852	◿		306	gold

Design was stitched on an 8½" x 8" piece of 14 count white Aida (design size 4¼" x 3⅝"). Three strands of floss were used for Cross Stitch and 1 strand for Backstitch.

Shown on page 11.

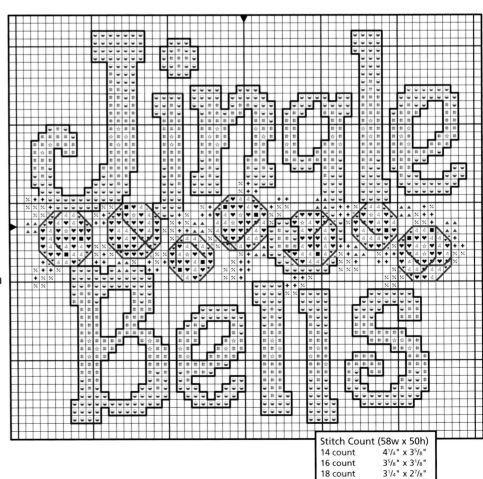

Stitch Count (58w x 50h)
14 count	4¼"	x 3⅝"
16 count	3⅝"	x 3⅛"
18 count	3¼"	x 2⅞"

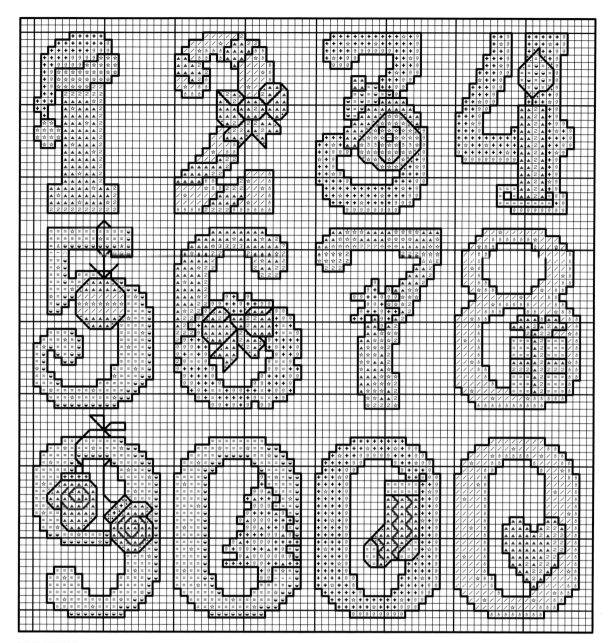

NUMBERS

X	DMC	¼X	B'ST	ANC.	COLOR
☆	blanc	✓		2	white
	310		✓	403	black
▲	321	✓		9046	red
③	353			6	peach
⑨	700	⑨		228	dk green
+	703	+		238	green

X	DMC	¼X	B'ST	ANC.	COLOR
=	726	=	✓	295	yellow
◔	729			890	gold
⑧	797			132	blue
✓	799	✓		136	lt blue
②	816			1005	maroon
−	970			316	orange

We used the numbers to stitch the holiday year on a 9" x 6" piece of 14 count white Aida (design size 5" x 1⁷/₈"). Three strands of floss were used for Cross Stitch and 1 strand for Backstitch.

Shown on page 6.

Personalize your project with Backstitch letters and numbers. Use 1 strand of floss for all Backstitches.

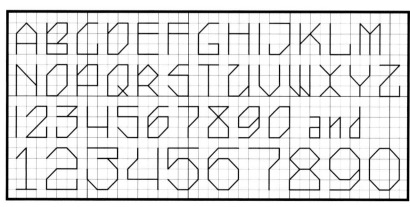

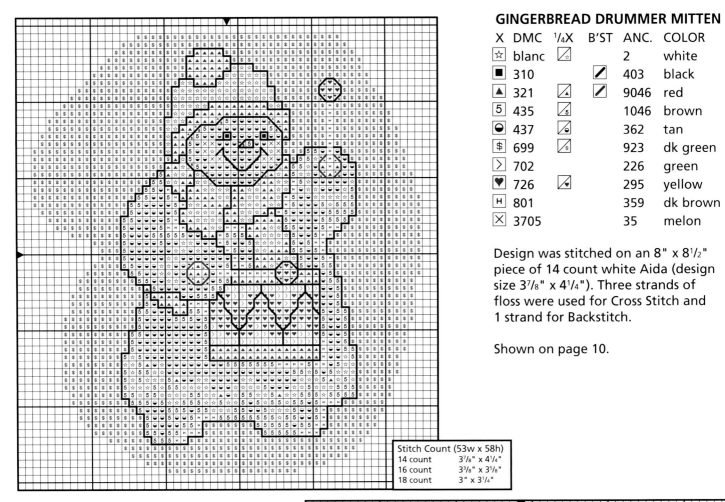

GINGERBREAD DRUMMER MITTEN

X	DMC	¼X	B'ST	ANC.	COLOR
☆	blanc	◹		2	white
■	310		╱	403	black
▲	321	◺	╱	9046	red
5	435	◹5		1046	brown
◖	437	◹		362	tan
$	699	◹s		923	dk green
>	702			226	green
♥	726	◹		295	yellow
H	801			359	dk brown
✕	3705			35	melon

Design was stitched on an 8" x 8½" piece of 14 count white Aida (design size 3⅞" x 4¼"). Three strands of floss were used for Cross Stitch and 1 strand for Backstitch.

Shown on page 10.

Stitch Count (53w x 58h)
14 count	3⅞"	x 4¼"
16 count	3⅜"	x 3⅝"
18 count	3"	x 3¼"

GINGERBREAD BUGLER MITTEN

X	DMC	¼X	B'ST	ANC.	COLOR
☆	blanc			2	white
■	310		╱	403	black
▲	321	◺	╱	9046	red
♥	435	◹		1046	brown
◖	437	◹		362	tan
$	699			923	dk green
=	726	◹=		295	yellow
H	801			359	dk brown
#	996	◹#		433	turquoise
✕	3705			35	melon

Design was stitched on an 8" x 8½" piece of 14 count white Aida (design size 3⅞" x 4¼"). Three strands of floss were used for Cross Stitch and 1 strand for Backstitch.

Shown on page 15.

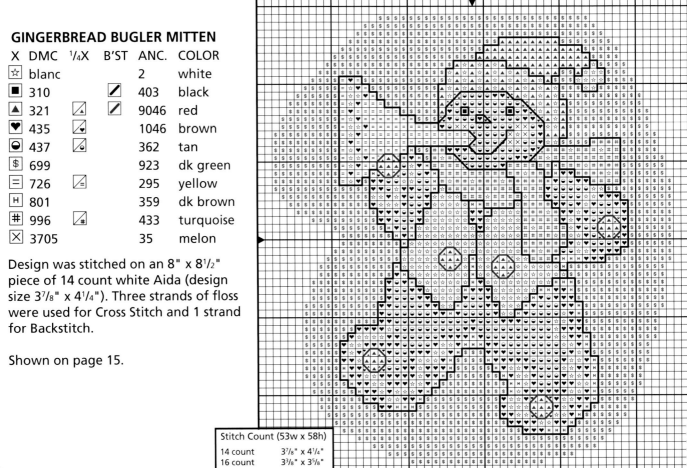

Stitch Count (53w x 58h)
14 count	3⅞"	x 4¼"
16 count	3⅜"	x 3⅝"
18 count	3"	x 3¼"

JOY ANGEL

X	DMC	¼X	B'ST	ANC.	COLOR
☆	blanc			2	white
♥	300		╱	352	brown
▲	321			9046	red
3	353	3		6	peach
◆	676			891	gold
	726		╱*	295	yellow
6	746	6		275	cream
	797		╱	132	dk blue
●	800			144	lt blue
#	809			130	blue
2	816	2	╱	1005	maroon
⊥	963			73	lt rose
✳	976			1001	dk gold
7	3705			35	melon
✕	3716			25	rose

*Use 2 strands.

Design was stitched on an 8½" x 8½" piece of 14 count white Aida (design size 4¼" x 4¼"). Three strands of floss were used for Cross Stitch and 1 strand for Backstitch unless otherwise noted.

Shown on page 15.

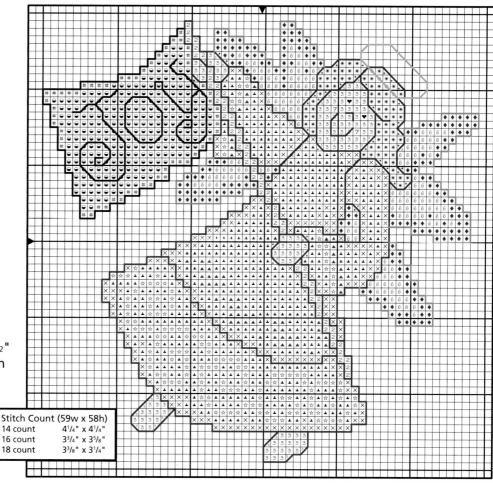

Stitch Count (59w x 58h)
14 count   4¼" x 4¼"
16 count   3¾" x 3⅝"
18 count   3⅜" x 3¼"

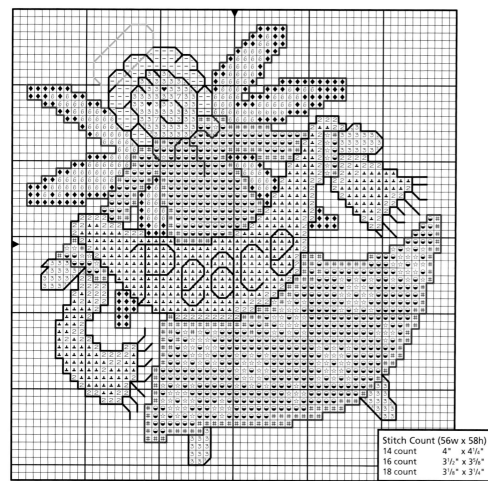

Stitch Count (56w x 58h)
14 count   4"   x 4¼"
16 count   3½" x 3⅝"
18 count   3⅛" x 3¼"

PEACE ANGEL

X	DMC	¼X	B'ST	ANC.	COLOR
☆	blanc			2	white
♥	300		╱	352	brown
3	353	3		6	peach
◆	676			891	gold
	726		╱*	295	yellow
6	746	6		275	cream
	797		╱	132	dk blue
●	800			144	lt blue
#	809			130	blue
⊥	963			73	lt rose
−	970			316	orange
7	3705			35	melon
2	3716	2		25	rose

*Use 2 strands.

Design was stitched on an 8" x 8½" piece of 14 count white Aida (design size 4" x 4¼"). Three strands of floss were used for Cross Stitch and 1 strand for Backstitch unless otherwise noted.

Shown on page 14.

CAROLING BOY

X	DMC	1/4X	B'ST	ANC.	COLOR
☆	blanc	⟋		2	white
m	318	⟋m		399	grey
▲	321	◢		9046	red
◗	352	◢		9	peach
3	353	⟋3		6	lt peach
✻	415	◢		398	lt grey
△	436	◢		1045	tan
⁒	701	⟋		227	green
✛	703	⟋⁺		238	lt green
=	726	⟋=		295	yellow
8	797	◢8	╱	132	dk blue
♥	798	◢♥		131	blue
⟋	799	⟋		136	lt blue
2	816	◢2		1005	maroon
■	3371	◢■	╱	382	black brown

Design was stitched on an 8" x 8¹⁄₂" piece of 14 count white Aida (design size 4" x 4¹⁄₄"). Three strands of floss were used for Cross Stitch and 1 strand for Backstitch.

Shown on page 15.

Stitch Count (56w x 59h)
14 count	4"	x 4¹⁄₄"
16 count	3¹⁄₂"	x 3³⁄₄"
18 count	3¹⁄₈"	x 3³⁄₈"

CAROLING GIRL

X	DMC	1/4X	B'ST	ANC.	COLOR
☆	blanc	⟋		2	white
✱	317			400	dk grey
m	318			399	grey
▲	321	◢		9046	red
◗	352	◢		9	peach
3	353	⟋3		6	lt peach
✻	415	⟋✻		398	lt grey
△	436	△		1045	tan
⁒	701	⟋⁒		227	green
✛	703	⟋⁺		238	lt green
	797		╱	132	dk blue
⟋	799	⟋		136	lt blue
2	816			1005	maroon
■	3371	◢■	╱	382	black brown

Design was stitched on an 8" x 8¹⁄₂" piece of 14 count white Aida (design size 4" x 4¹⁄₄"). Three strands of floss were used for Cross Stitch and 1 strand for Backstitch.

Shown on page 15.

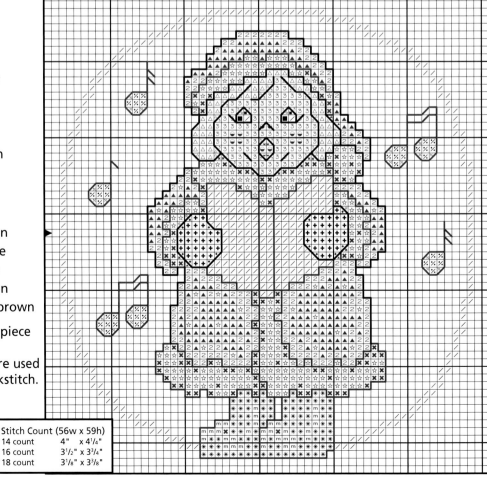

Stitch Count (56w x 59h)
14 count	4"	x 4¹⁄₄"
16 count	3¹⁄₂"	x 3³⁄₄"
18 count	3¹⁄₈"	x 3³⁄₈"

HAPPY SANTA

X	DMC	¼X	B'ST	ANC.	COLOR
☆	blanc	◪		2	white
■	310		✎	403	black
▲	321			9046	red
★	352			9	peach
③	353	◪		6	lt peach
◆	415			398	lt grey
◕	701	◪		227	green
✚	703			238	lt green
═	726	◪		295	yellow
②	816		✎	1005	maroon

Design was stitched on a 7½" x 8½" piece of 14 count white Aida (design size 3½" x 4½"). Three strands of floss were used for Cross Stitch and 1 strand for Backstitch.

Shown on page 13.

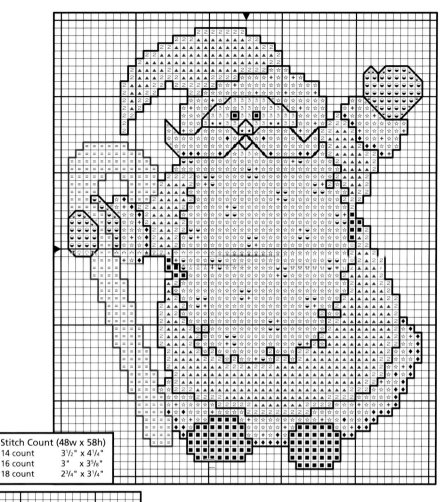

Stitch Count (48w x 58h)		
14 count	3½"	x 4¼"
16 count	3"	x 3⅝"
18 count	2¾"	x 3¼"

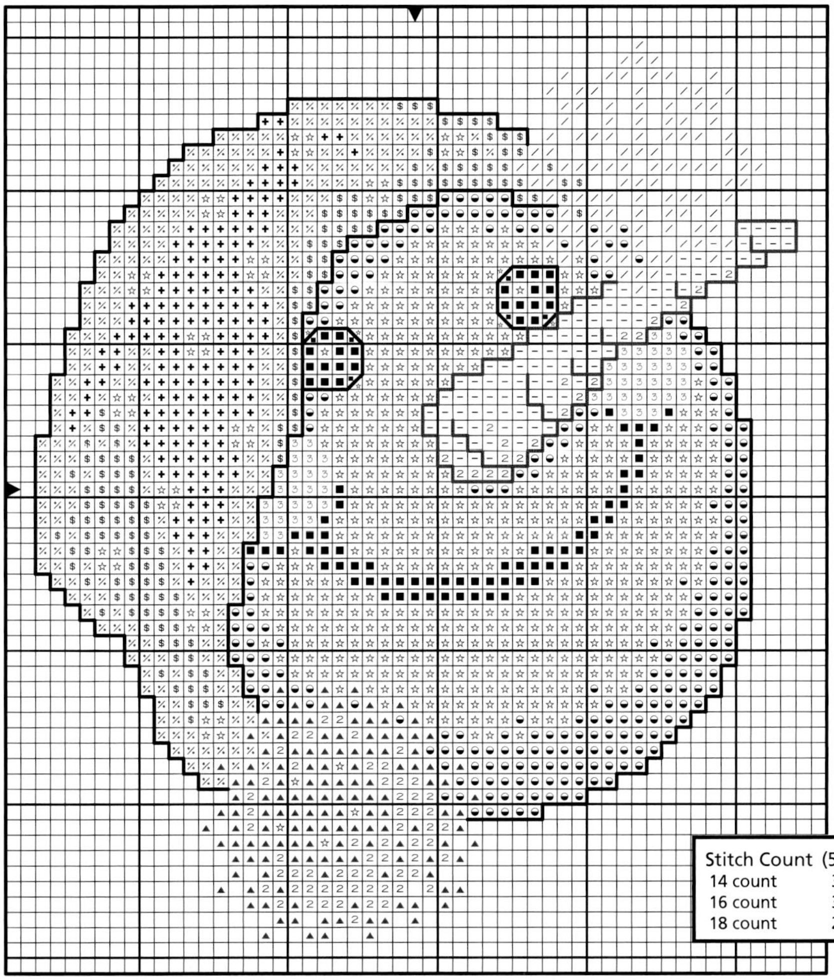

SNOWMAN HEAD

X	DMC	¼X	B'ST	ANC.	COLOR
☆	blanc	◪		2	white
■	310	◪	✎	403	black
▲	321			9046	red
③	353			6	peach
$	699			923	dk green
⁒	701			227	green
✚	703			238	lt green
◕	762			234	lt grey
╱	799			136	blue
②	816		✎	1005	maroon
═	970			316	orange

Design was stitched on an 8" x 8½" piece of 14 count white Aida (design size 3¾" x 4¼"). Three strands of floss were used for Cross Stitch and 1 strand for Backstitch.

Shown on page 13.

Stitch Count (51w x 59h)		
14 count	3¾"	x 4¼"
16 count	3¼"	x 3¾"
18 count	2⅞"	x 3⅜"

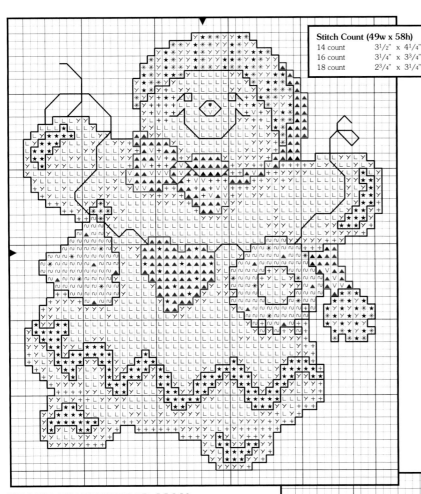

GINGERBREAD LADY WITH GARLAND

X	DMC	1/4X	B'ST	ANC.	COLOR
★	blanc			2	white
▲	321			9046	red
V	351			10	peach
+	352			9	lt peach
+	434			310	golden brown
Y	436			1045	dk beige
L	437	/L		362	beige
✳	726			295	yellow
V	801	/⟋	/	359	brown
▲	816		/	1005	maroon
✳	826			161	blue
Y	827			160	lt blue
∩	988			243	green
●	blanc			2	white Fr. Knot

Design was stitched on a 7¹/₂" x 8¹/₂" piece of 14 count white Aida (design size 3¹/₂" x 4¹/₄"). Three strands of floss were used for Cross Stitch and 1 strand for Backstitch and French Knots.

Shown on page 10.

HEART GINGERBREAD MAN

X	DMC	1/4X	B'ST	ANC.	COLOR
☆	blanc	/☆		2	white
Z	321			9046	red
Z	351	/z		10	peach
+	352			9	lt peach
+	434			310	golden brown
C	436	/c		1045	dk beige
L	437	/L		362	beige
✳	726	/✳		295	yellow
★	783			306	gold
▲	801	/▲	/	359	brown
▲	816			1005	maroon
✳	826			161	blue
△	827			160	lt blue
■	987			244	lt green
C	989	/c		242	dk green
●	blanc			2	white Fr. Knot

Design was stitched on an 8" x 8¹/₂" piece of 14 count white Aida (design size 4" x 4¹/₂"). Three strands of floss were used for Cross Stitch and 1 strand for Backstitch and French Knots.

Shown on page 8.

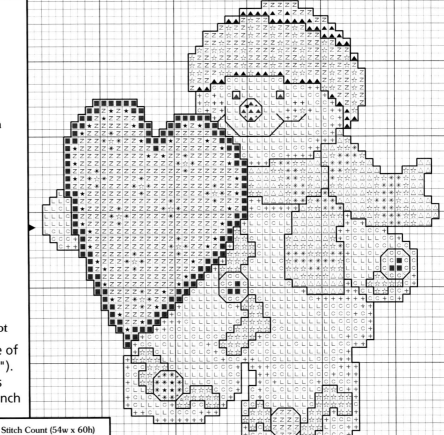

HEART GINGERBREAD LADY

X	DMC	1/4X	B'ST	ANC.	COLOR
★	blanc			2	white
Z	321			9046	red
Z	351			10	peach
+	352			9	lt peach
+	434			310	golden brown
✳	436			1045	dk beige
L	437	◹		362	beige
✳	702			226	lime green
Z	775			128	baby blue
L	801	◹	◺	359	brown
▲	816			1005	maroon
●	blanc			2	white Fr. Knot

Design was stitched on an 8" x 8 1/2" piece of 14 count white Aida (design size 4" x 4 1/4"). Three strands of floss were used for Cross Stitch and 1 strand for Backstitch and French Knots.

Shown on page 8.

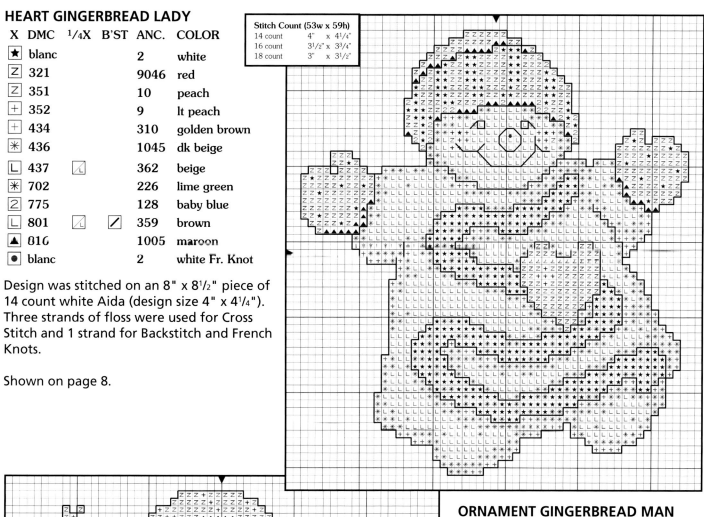

Stitch Count (53w x 59h)		
14 count	4"	x 4 1/4"
16 count	3 1/2"	x 3 3/4"
18 count	3"	x 3 1/2"

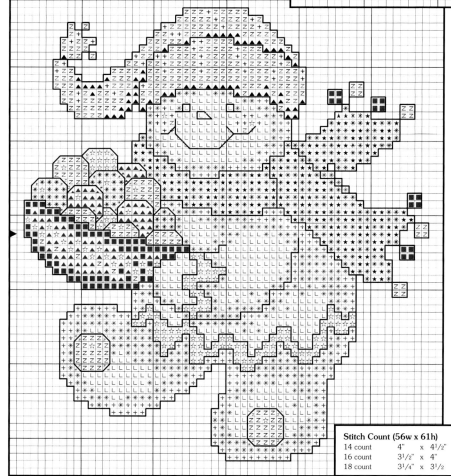

Stitch Count (56w x 61h)		
14 count	4"	x 4 1/2"
16 count	3 1/2"	x 4"
18 count	3 1/4"	x 3 1/2

ORNAMENT GINGERBREAD MAN

X	DMC	1/4X	B'ST	ANC.	COLOR
☆	blanc	◹	◹	2	white
Z	321		◹	9046	red
Z	351			10	peach
+	352			9	lt peach
+	434			310	golden brown
✳	436		◹	1045	dk beige
L	437	◹		362	beige
✳	726		◹	295	yellow
★	783			306	gold
L	801	◹	◺	359	brown
▲	816			1005	maroon
■	987			244	green
▲	989	◹		242	dk green

Design was stitched on an 8" x 8 1/2" piece of 14 count white Aida (design size 4" x 4 1/2"). Three strands of floss were used for Cross Stitch and 1 strand for Backstitch.

Shown on page 10.

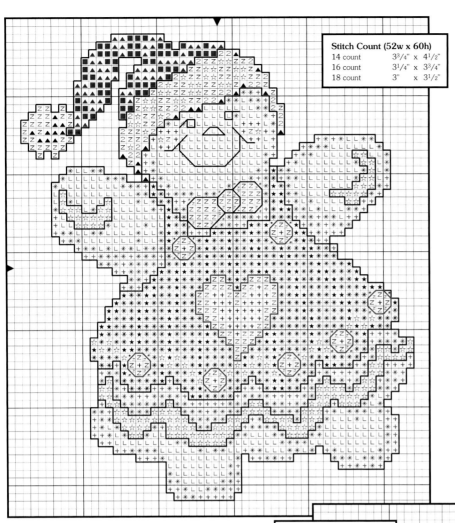

Stitch Count (52w x 60h)
14 count	3³/₄"	x 4¹/₂"
16 count	3¹/₄"	x 3³/₄"
18 count	3"	x 3¹/₂"

GINGERBREAD LADY WITH APRON

X	DMC	1/4X	B'ST	ANC.	COLOR
☆	blanc			2	white
Z	321	z		9046	red
Z	351			10	peach
+	352			9	lt peach
+	434			310	golden brown
✳	436	✳		1045	dk beige
L	437	L		362	beige
✳	726	✳		295	yellow
2	775			128	baby blue
★	783	★		306	gold
L	801	L	/	359	brown
▲	816		/	1005	maroon
■	987			244	green
▲	989			242	dk green

Design was stitched on an 8" x 8¹/₂" piece of 14 count white Aida (design size 3³/₄" x 4¹/₂"). Three strands of floss were used for Cross Stitch and 1 strand for Backstitch.

Shown on page 8.

CANDY CANE GINGERBREAD MAN

X	DMC	1/4X	B'ST	ANC.	COLOR
☆	blanc			2	white
Z	321	z	/	9046	red
Z	351			10	peach
+	352			9	lt peach
+	434			310	golden brown
✳	436	✳		1045	dk beige
L	437	L		362	beige
✳	726	✳		295	yellow
2	775			128	baby blue
★	783	★		306	gold
L	801	L	/	359	brown
■	987	■		244	green
▲	989	▲		242	dk green
●	blanc			2	white Fr. Knot

Design was stitched on a 7¹/₂" x 8" piece of 14 count white Aida (design size 3¹/₂" x 4"). Three strands of floss were used for Cross Stitch and 1 strand for Backstitch and French Knots.

Shown on page 8.

Stitch Count (48w x 55h)
14 count	3¹/₂"	x 4"
16 count	3"	x 3¹/₂"
18 count	2³/₄"	x 3¹/₄"

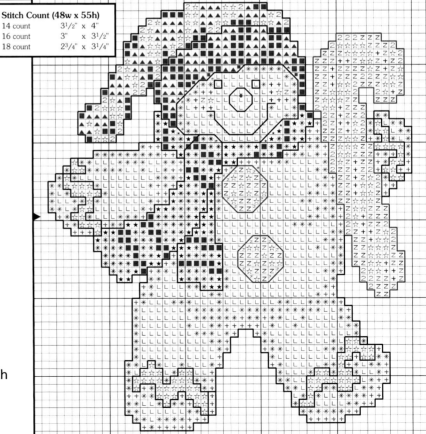

GINGERBREAD HOUSE

X	DMC	¼X	B'ST	ANC.	COLOR
☆	blanc	◿		2	white
	310		✎	403	black
▲	321	◿	✎	9046	red
✖	415			398	lt grey
⚡	434			310	brown
△	436			1045	tan
%	701			227	green
+	703	◿		238	lt green
@	738			361	lt tan
7	3705			35	melon

Design was stitched on an 8" x 7½" piece of 14 count white Aida (design size 4" x 3½"). Three strands of floss were used for Cross Stitch and 1 strand for Backstitch.

Shown on page 11.

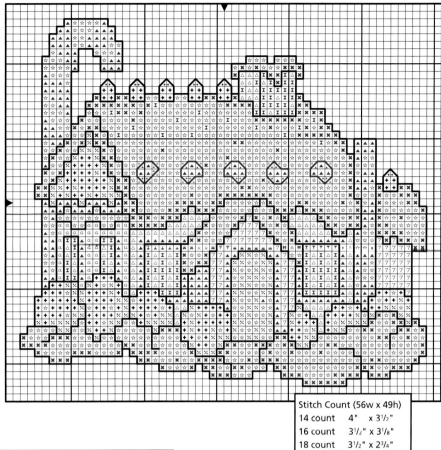

Stitch Count (56w x 49h)
14 count	4"	x 3½"
16 count	3½"	x 3⅛"
18 count	3½"	x 2¾"

Stitch Count (53w x 60h)
14 count	4"	x 4½"
16 count	3½"	x 3¾"
18 count	3"	x 3½"

I LOVE SNOW DOG

X	DMC	¼X	B'ST	ANC.	COLOR
☆	blanc			2	white
▲	310	◿	✎	403	black
■	321	◿		9046	red
+	351	◿		10	dk peach
+	352	◿		9	peach
♥	435	◿		1046	golden brown
L	437	◿		362	beige
☆	702	◿		226	lt green
✳	712	◿		926	cream
✳	739	◿		387	dk cream
▲	816	◿	✎	1005	maroon
■	898			360	brown
♥	920	◿		1004	orange
2	3841			9159	baby blue
●	blanc			2	white Fr. Knot

Design was stitched on an 8" x 8½" piece of 14 count white Aida (design size 4" x 4½"). Three strands of floss were used for Cross Stitch and 1 strand for Backstitch and French Knots.

Shown on page 9.

43

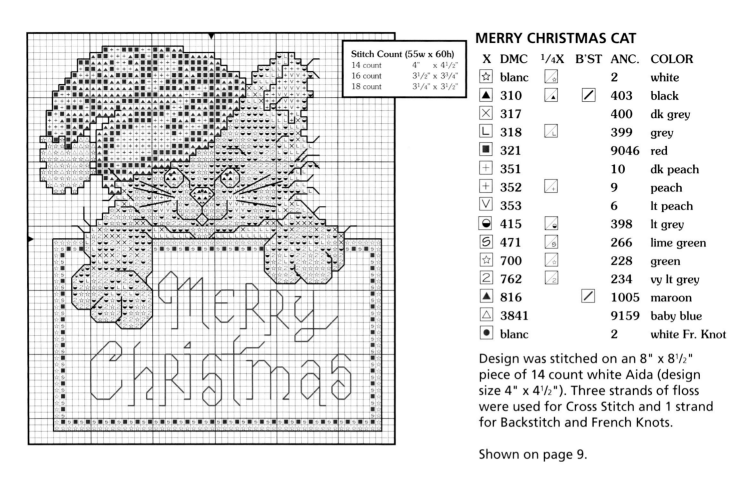

MERRY CHRISTMAS CAT

X	DMC	1/4X	B'ST	ANC.	COLOR
☆	blanc	◹		2	white
▲	310	◿	╱	403	black
✕	317			400	dk grey
∟	318	◹		399	grey
■	321			9046	red
+	351			10	dk peach
+	352	◿		9	peach
∨	353			6	lt peach
◕	415	◹		398	lt grey
S	471	◿		266	lime green
☆	700	◹		228	green
2	762	◿		234	vy lt grey
▲	816		╱	1005	maroon
△	3841			9159	baby blue
●	blanc			2	white Fr. Knot

Design was stitched on an 8" x 8½" piece of 14 count white Aida (design size 4" x 4½"). Three strands of floss were used for Cross Stitch and 1 strand for Backstitch and French Knots.

Shown on page 9.

Stitch Count (55w x 60h)
14 count	4"	x 4½"
16 count	3½"	x 3¾"
18 count	3¼"	x 3½"

SKATING SANTA

X	DMC	1/4X	B'ST	ANC.	COLOR
☆	blanc	◹		2	white
▲	310	◿	╱	403	black
✕	318	◿		399	grey
■	321	◿		9046	red
+	351			10	dk peach
+	352	◿		9	peach
∨	353			6	lt peach
∟	414			235	dk grey
2	415	◿		398	lt grey
☆	702			226	green
✕	726			295	yellow
▲	816	◿		1005	maroon
e	930			1035	blue
★	3852			306	dk gold

Design was stitched on a 7½" x 8½" piece of 14 count white Aida (design size 3¼" x 4¼"). Three strands of floss were used for Cross Stitch and 1 strand for Backstitch.

Shown on page 8.

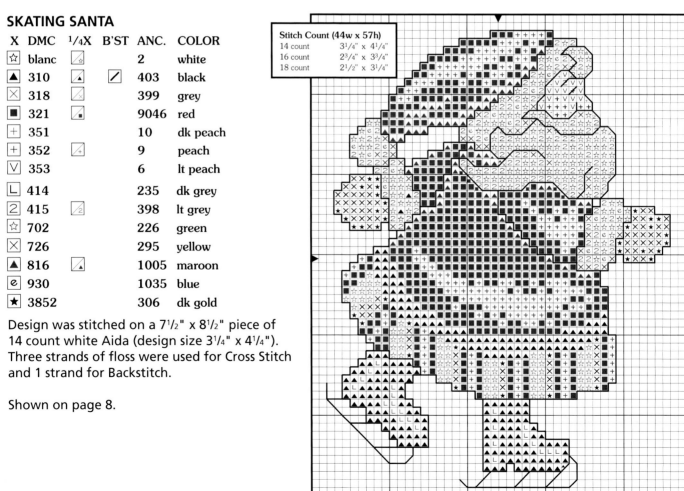

Stitch Count (44w x 57h)
14 count	3¼"	x 4¼"
16 count	2¾"	x 3¾"
18 count	2½"	x 3¼"

HAPPY HOLIDAYS SANTA

X	DMC	1/4X	B'ST	ANC.	COLOR
☆	blanc	◹		2	white
▲	310		╱	403	black
■	321	◢		9046	red
+	352	⊹		9	peach
V	353	◹		6	lt peach
✕	414			235	dk grey
◗	415			398	lt grey
✳	677	⊹		886	lt gold
☆	701		╱	227	dk green
C	704	◹		256	lime green
2	762	◿		234	vy lt grey
▲	816	◹		1005	maroon

Stitch Count (51w x 56h)
14 count	3 3/4"	x 4"
16 count	3 1/4"	x 3 1/2"
18 count	3"	x 3 1/4"

Design was stitched on an 8" x 8" piece of 14 count white Aida (design size 3 3/4" x 4"). Three strands of floss were used for Cross Stitch and 1 strand for Backstitch.

Shown on page 15.

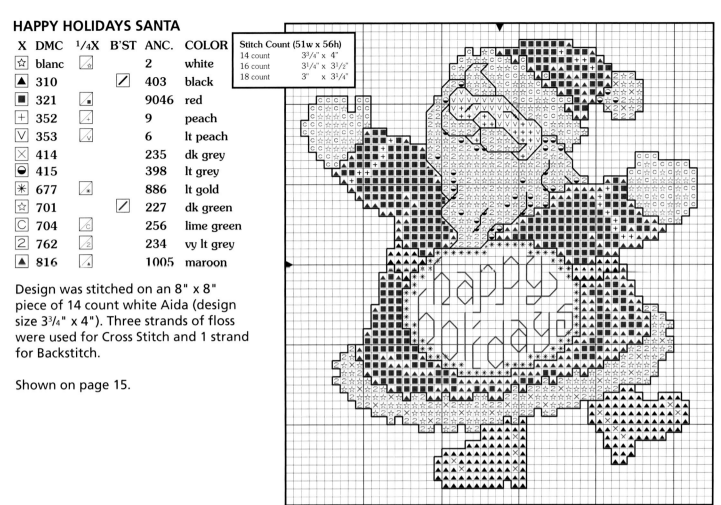

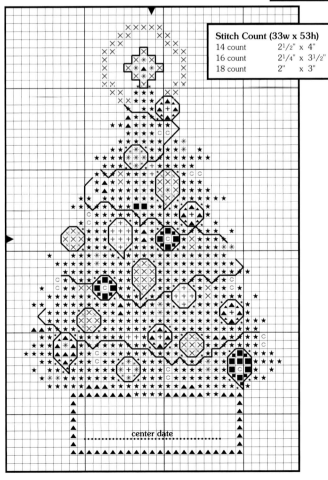

Stitch Count (33w x 53h)
14 count	2 1/2"	x 4"
16 count	2 1/4"	x 3 1/2"
18 count	2"	x 3"

center date

TREE

X	DMC	1/4X	B'ST	ANC.	COLOR
+	164	◹			sea green
	310		╱	403	black
▲	321	◢		9046	dk red
+	352			9	peach
★	702	◹		226	lime green
✕	726	◹		295	yellow
■	798	◢		131	blue
C	809			130	lt blue
✳	947	◹		330	orange

Design was stitched on a 6 1/2" x 8" piece of 14 count white Aida (design size 2 1/2" x 4"). Three strands of floss were used for Cross Stitch and 1 strand for Backstitch. Personalize using numbers chart #2 on page 35.

Shown on page 6.

BOY BOOTIES

X	DMC	1/4X	B'ST	ANC.	COLOR
■	351			10	dk peach
	817		/	13	red
▲	911	◺		205	green
+	913			204	lt green
2	955			206	vy lt green
■	3818	◾	/	923	dk green

Design was stitched on a 7½" x 7½" piece of 14 count white Aida (design size 3½" x 3½"). Three strands of floss were used for Cross Stitch and 1 strand for Backstitch. Personalize using Backstitch letters and numbers on page 35.

Shown on page 9.

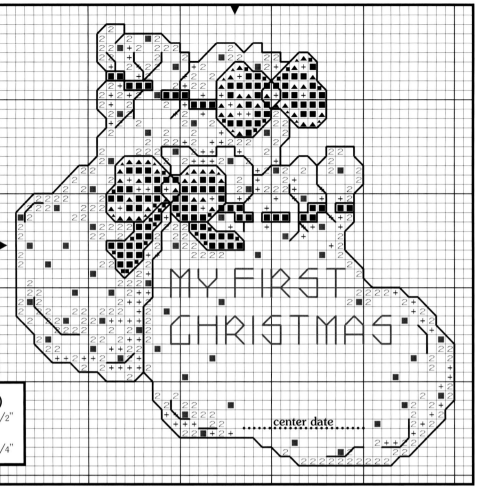

Stitch Count (48w x 47h)

14 count	3½" x	3½"
16 count	3" x	3"
18 count	2¾" x	2¾"

Stitch Count (34w x 38h)

14 count	2½" x	2¾"
16 count	2¼" x	2½"
18 count	2" x	2¼"

SNOWMAN WITH STAR

X	DMC	1/4X	B'ST	ANC.	COLOR
☆	blanc			2	white
C	310		/	403	black
■	321	◾		9046	red
+	351			10	dk peach
●	353			6	peach
▲	700			228	green
✕	702	◿		226	dk lime green
C	704	c		256	lime green
✕	726	◿		295	dk yellow
—	746	◿		275	lt yellow
▲	816			1005	maroon
+	920		/	1004	rust
2	3841	◿		9159	baby blue

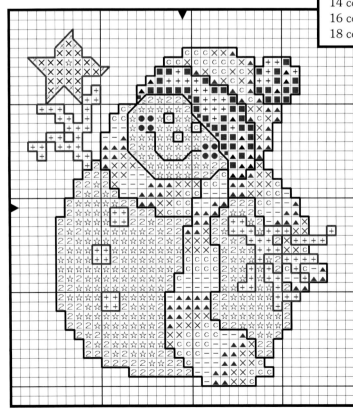

Design was stitched on a 6½" x 7" piece of 14 count white Aida (design size 2½" x 2¾"). Three strands of floss were used for Cross Stitch and 1 strand for Backstitch.

Shown on page 6.

GIRL BOOTIES

X DMC	1/4X	B'ST	ANC.	COLOR
■ 321	▨	╱	9046	dk red
C 351	⊠		10	dk peach
✚ 352			9	peach
✚ 353			6	lt peach
a 955			206	vy lt green
3818		╱	923	dk green

Design was stitched on a 7¹/₂" x 7¹/₂" piece of 14 count white Aida (design size 3¹/₂" x 3¹/₂"). Three strands of floss were used for Cross Stitch and 1 strand for Backstitch. Personalize using Backstitch letters and numbers on page 35.

Shown on page 9.

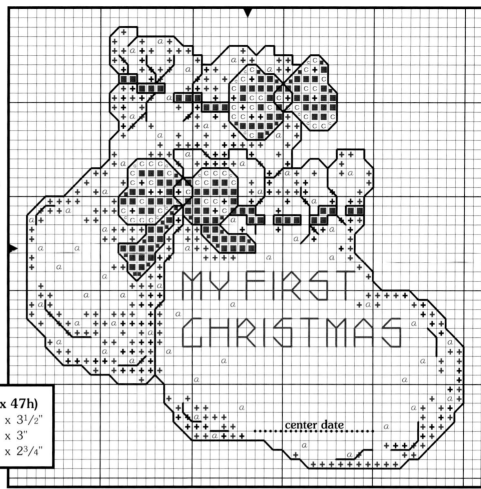

Stitch Count (48w x 47h)
14 count	3¹/₂"	x 3¹/₂"
16 count	3"	x 3"
18 count	2³/₄"	x 2³/₄"

Stitch Count (39w x 39h)
14 count	3"	x 3"
16 count	2¹/₂"	x 2¹/₂"
18 count	2¹/₄"	x 2¹/₄"

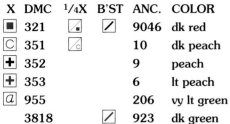

SNOWMAN WITH LIGHTS

X DMC	1/4X	B'ST	ANC.	COLOR
☆ blanc			2	white
▲ 310		╱	403	black
2 321	▨		9046	red
✚ 351			10	dk peach
✕ 353			6	peach
☆ 677			886	gold
✳ 701		╱	227	lt green
✕ 726			295	dk yellow
▲ 798	▨		131	blue
5 809			130	lt blue
♥ 920		╱	1004	rust
✚ 947			330	orange
2 3841	▨		9159	baby blue

Design was stitched on a 7" x 7" piece of 14 count white Aida (design size 3" x 3"). Three strands of floss were used for Cross Stitch and 1 strand for Backstitch.

Shown on page 7.

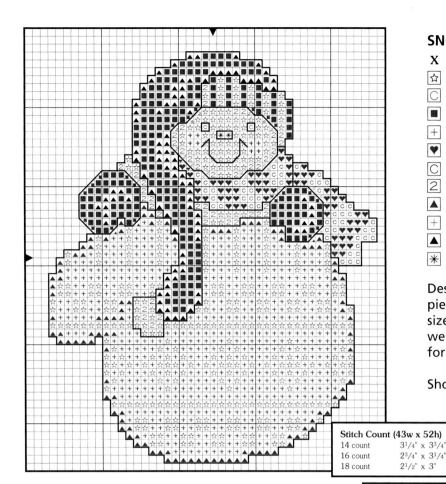

SNOWMAN IN MITTEN

X	DMC	1/4X	B'ST	ANC.	COLOR
☆	white	☆		2	white
C	310		/	403	black
■	321	▪		9046	red
+	353			6	peach
♥	700	♥		228	green
C	704	c		256	lt lime green
2	775	2		128	baby blue
▲	796	▲		133	dk blue
+	798			131	blue
▲	816			1005	maroon
✳	947			330	orange

Design was stitched on a 7¼" x 7¾" piece of 14 count white Aida (design size 3¼" x 3¾"). Three strands of floss were used for Cross Stitch and 1 strand for Backstitch.

Shown on page 15.

Stitch Count (43w x 52h)
14 count	3¼" x 3¾"
16 count	2¾" x 3¼"
18 count	2½" x 3"

SNOWMAN IN STOCKING

X	DMC	1/4X	B'ST	ANC.	COLOR
☆	blanc			2	white
C	164				sea green
C	310		/	403	black
■	321			9046	red
+	353			6	peach
▲	700			228	green
+	702	+		226	dk lime green
−	704			256	lime green
×	726	×		295	dk yellow
S	727			293	yellow
2	775	2		128	lt baby blue
▲	816			1005	maroon
✳	947			330	orange

Design was stitched on a 7" x 8¼" piece of 14 count white Aida (design size 3" x 4¼"). Three strands of floss were used for Cross Stitch and 1 strand for Backstitch.

Shown on page 7.

Stitch Count (41w x 57h)
14 count	3" x 4¼"
16 count	2¾" x 3¾"
18 count	2½" x 3¼"

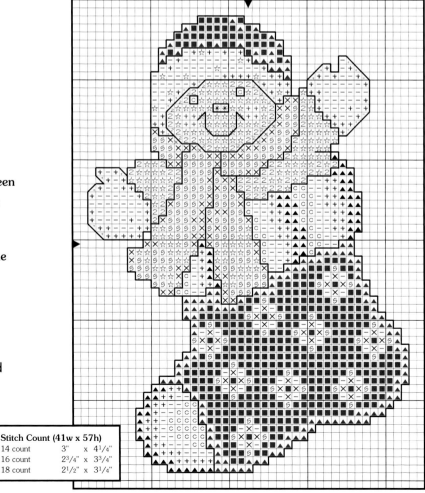

HAPPY HOLIDAYS SNOWMAN

X	DMC	¼X	B'ST	ANC.	COLOR
☆	white	☆		2	white
C	310	c	/	403	black
■	321			9046	red
+	351			10	dk peach
+	353			6	peach
▲	433			358	brown
♥	700		/	228	green
♥	702	♥		226	lime green
C	704			256	lt lime green
X	726	X		295	yellow
X	746			275	cream
2	775	2		128	baby blue
✳	932	✳		1033	blue grey
▲	3820	▲		306	gold

Design was stitched on an 8" x 8" piece of 14 count red Aida (design size 3³/₄" x 4"). Three strands of floss were used for Cross Stitch and 1 strand for Backstitch.

Shown on page 8.

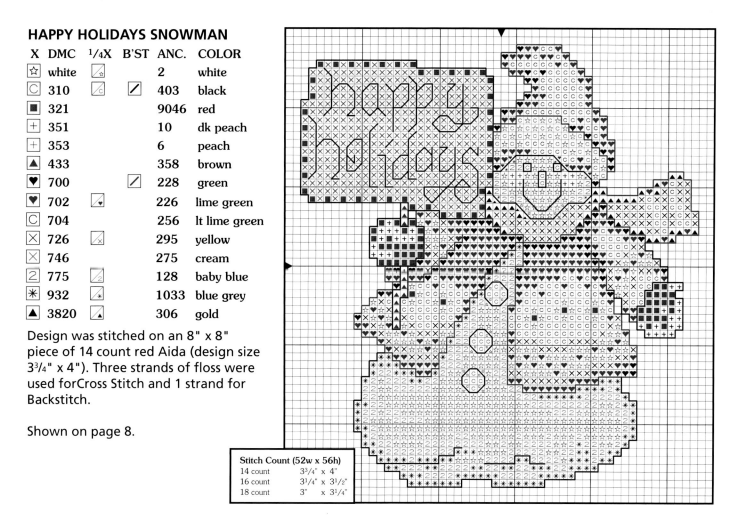

Stitch Count (52w x 56h)	
14 count	3³/₄" x 4"
16 count	3¹/₄" x 3¹/₂"
18 count	3" x 3¹/₄"

Stitch Count (56w x 48h)	
14 count	4" x 3¹/₂"
16 count	3¹/₂" x 3"
18 count	3¹/₄" x 2³/₄"

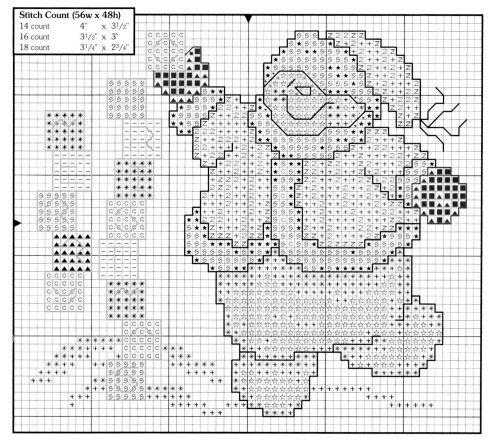

MERRY CHRISTMAS SNOWMAN

X	DMC	¼X	B'ST	ANC.	COLOR
☆	white	☆		2	white
C	164				sea green
C	310	c	/	403	black
■	321	■		9046	red
✳	353			6	peach
▲	677			886	lt gold
S	726	S		295	yellow
−	746			275	cream
+	775		/	128	baby blue
Z	796			133	dk blue
+	798			131	blue
2	809			130	lt blue
▲	816		/	1005	maroon
	895		/	1044	green
✳	932			1033	blue grey
★	3852	★		306	dk gold

Design was stitched on an 8" x 7¹/₂" piece of 14 count white Aida (design size 4" x 3¹/₂"). Three strands of floss were used for Cross Stitch and 1 strand for Backstitch.

Shown on page 8.

49

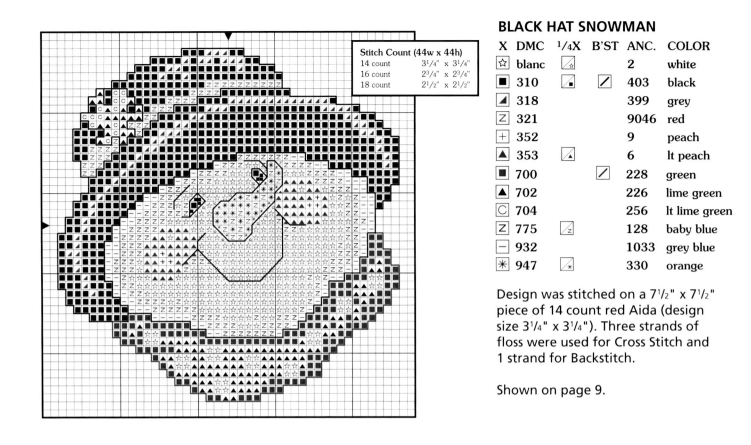

BLACK HAT SNOWMAN

X	DMC	¼X	B'ST	ANC.	COLOR
☆	blanc	☆		2	white
■	310	■	/	403	black
◢	318			399	grey
Z	321			9046	red
+	352			9	peach
▲	353	◢		6	lt peach
■	700		/	228	green
▲	702			226	lime green
C	704			256	lt lime green
Z	775	z		128	baby blue
−	932			1033	grey blue
✳	947	✳		330	orange

Design was stitched on a 7½" x 7½" piece of 14 count red Aida (design size 3¼" x 3¼"). Three strands of floss were used for Cross Stitch and 1 strand for Backstitch.

Shown on page 9.

RED HAT SNOWMAN

X	DMC	¼X	B'ST	ANC.	COLOR
☆	blanc	☆		2	white
■	310		/	403	black
■	321			9046	red
+	352			9	peach
−	353			6	lt peach
▲	436			1045	golden brown
✳	739			387	beige
2	775	2		128	baby blue
▲	816		/	1005	maroon
+	932			1033	grey blue
✳	947	✳		330	orange

Design was stitched on a 7" x 8" piece of 14 count white Aida (design size 2¾" x 3¾"). Three strands of floss were used for Cross Stitch and 1 strand for Backstitch.

Shown on page 6.

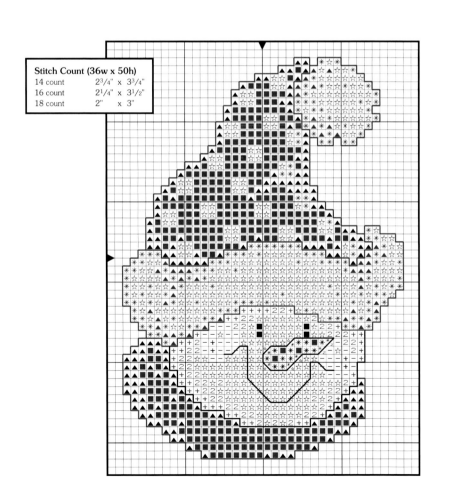

STRIPED CAP SNOWMAN

X	DMC	¼X	B'ST	ANC.	COLOR
☆	blanc	☆		2	white
Z	310	z	╱	403	black
C	318	c		399	grey
▲	321	▲		9046	red
C	351			10	dk peach
+	352	+		9	peach
−	353			6	lt peach
+	739			387	beige
Z	762	z		234	lt grey
▲	775	▲		128	baby blue
■	816	■	╱	1005	maroon
−	932	−		1033	grey blue
✳	947	✳		330	orange
●	310			403	black Fr. Knot

Stitch Count (40w x 47h)	
14 count	3" x 3½"
16 count	2½" x 3"
18 count	2¼" x 2¾"

Design was stitched on a 7" x 7½" piece of 14 count white Aida (design size 3" x 3½"). Three strands of floss were used for Cross Stitch and 1 strand for Backstitch and French Knots.

Shown on page 6.

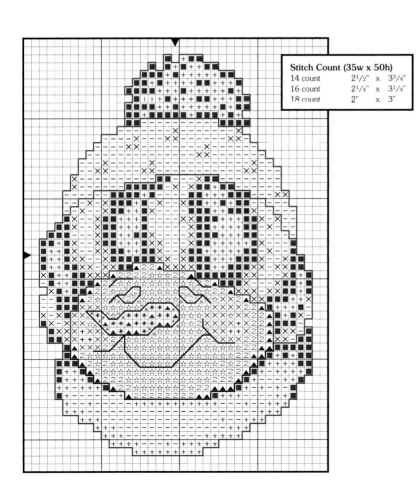

Stitch Count (35w x 50h)	
14 count	2½" x 3¾"
16 count	2¼" x 3¼"
18 count	2" x 3"

GREEN HAT SNOWMAN

X	DMC	¼X	B'ST	ANC.	COLOR
☆	blanc	☆		2	white
2	310	2	╱	403	black
▲	321			9046	red
+	352			9	peach
⊠	353	⊠		6	lt peach
■	700			228	green
+	702			226	lime green
−	704			256	lt lime green
⊠	726			295	dk yellow
−	727			293	yellow
2	775	2		128	baby blue
	895		╱	1044	dk green
▲	932			1033	grey blue
✳	947	✳		330	orange

Design was stitched on a 6½" x 8" piece of 14 count red Aida (design size 2½" x 3¾"). Three strands of floss were used for Cross Stitch and 1 strand for Backstitch.

Shown on page 7.

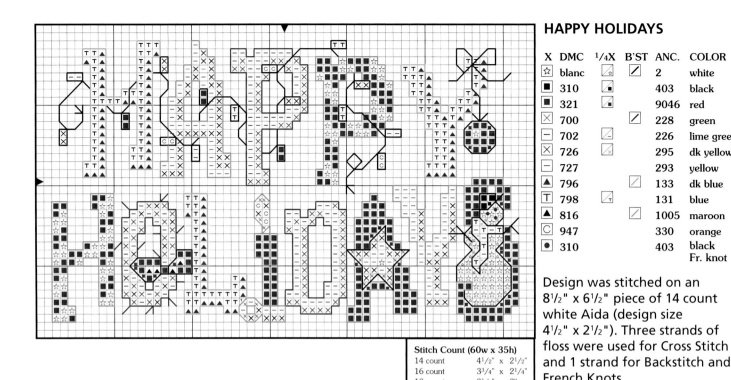

HAPPY HOLIDAYS

X	DMC	1/4X	B'ST	ANC.	COLOR
☆	blanc	◹	/	2	white
■	310	◾	/	403	black
■	321	◾	/	9046	red
✕	700		/	228	green
─	702	◹		226	lime green
✕	726	◹		295	dk yellow
─	727			293	yellow
▲	796	◹		133	dk blue
T	798	◹		131	blue
▲	816		/	1005	maroon
C	947			330	orange
●	310			403	black Fr. knot

Design was stitched on an 8 1/2" x 6 1/2" piece of 14 count white Aida (design size 4 1/2" x 2 1/2"). Three strands of floss were used for Cross Stitch and 1 strand for Backstitch and French Knots.

Shown on page 6.

Stitch Count (60w x 35h)

14 count	4 1/2"	x 2 1/2"
16 count	3 3/4"	x 2 1/4"
18 count	3 1/2"	x 2"

I LOVE SNOW

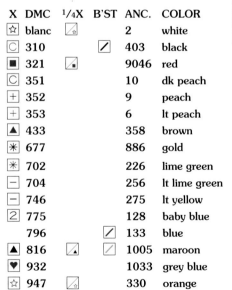

X	DMC	1/4X	B'ST	ANC.	COLOR
☆	blanc	◹		2	white
C	310		/	403	black
■	321	◾		9046	red
C	351			10	dk peach
+	352			9	peach
+	353			6	lt peach
▲	433			358	brown
✳	677			886	gold
✳	702			226	lime green
─	704			256	lt lime green
─	746			275	lt yellow
2	775			128	baby blue
	796		/	133	blue
▲	816	◹	/	1005	maroon
♥	932			1033	grey blue
☆	947	◹		330	orange

Design was stitched on an 8" x 8" piece of 14 count white Aida (design size 3 3/4" x 4"). Three strands of floss were used for Cross Stitch and 1 strand for Backstitch.

Shown on page 7.

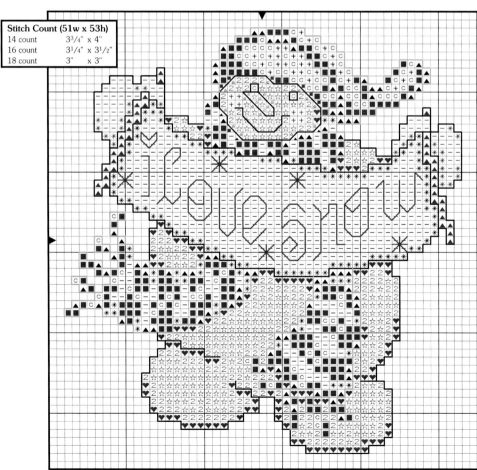

Stitch Count (51w x 53h)

14 count	3 3/4"	x 4"
16 count	3 1/4"	x 3 1/2"
18 count	3"	x 3"

Stitch Count (41w x 37h)

14 count	3"	x 2³/₄"
16 count	2³/₄"	x 2¹/₂"
18 count	2¹/₂"	x 2¹/₄"

Design was stitched on a 7" x 7" piece of 14 count white Aida (design size 3" x 2³/₄"). Three strands of floss were used for Cross Stitch and 1 strand for Backstitch.

Shown on page 9.

HAT

X	DMC	B'ST	ANC.	COLOR
☆	blanc		2	white
■	321	╱	9046	red
C	351		10	peach
▲	796	╱	133	blue
2	809		130	lt blue

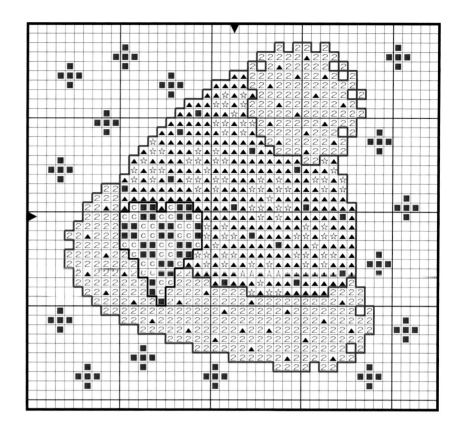

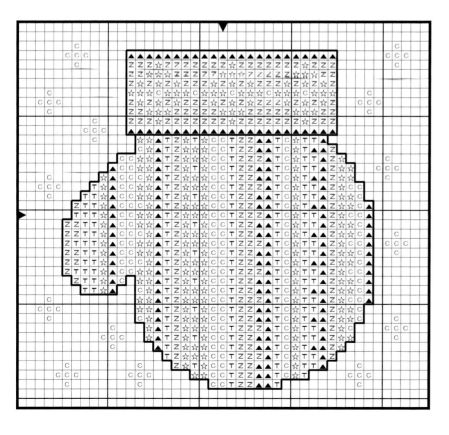

Stitch Count (41w x 37h)

14 count	3"	x 2³/₄"
16 count	2³/₄"	x 2¹/₂"
18 count	2¹/₂"	x 2¹/₄"

Design was stitched on a 7" x 7" piece of 14 count white Aida (design size 3" x 2³/₄"). Three strands of floss were used for Cross Stitch and 1 strand for Backstitch.

Shown on page 9.

MITTEN

X	DMC	B'ST	ANC.	COLOR
☆	blanc		2	white
Z	321		9046	red
C	704		256	lime green
▲	796	╱	133	blue
T	809		130	lt blue

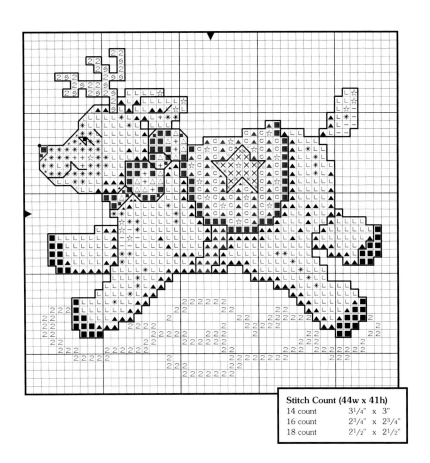

Stitch Count (44w x 41h)

14 count	3¼"	x	3"
16 count	2¾"	x	2¾"
18 count	2½"	x	2½"

FLYING REINDEER

X	DMC	¼X	B'ST	ANC.	COLOR
☆	blanc			2	white
■	321	▪	/	9046	red
△	351			10	dk peach
+	352			9	peach
▲	435	◢		1046	golden brown
L	437	◿		362	beige
▲	702	◢		226	green
C	704	◿		256	lime green
✕	726	◿		295	yellow
✳	739	◿		387	beige
−	746			275	lt yellow
⊿	775			128	baby blue
Ϩ	809			130	blue
■	3371	▪	/	382	dk brown
●	blanc			2	white Fr. Knot

Design was stitched on a 7¼" x 7" piece of 14 count white Aida (design size 3¼" x 3"). Three strands of floss were used for Cross Stitch and 1 strand for Backstitch and French Knots.

Shown on page 6.

WREATH

X	DMC	¼X	B'ST	ANC.	COLOR
☆	blanc			2	white
	310		/	403	black
▲	321			9046	red
−	350			11	peach
+	352			9	lt peach
✕	726			295	yellow
★	782	◢		307	gold
−	798			131	blue
■	816			1005	maroon
■	3346	▪		267	dk avocado green
+	3347	◿		266	avocado green

Design was stitched on a 7¾" x 7¾" piece of 14 count white Aida (design size 3¾" x 3¾"). Three strands of floss were used for Cross Stitch and 1 strand for Backstitch.

Shown on page 10.

Stitch Count (51w x 50h)

14 count	3¾"	x	3¾"
16 count	3¼"	x	3¼"
18 count	3"	x	3"

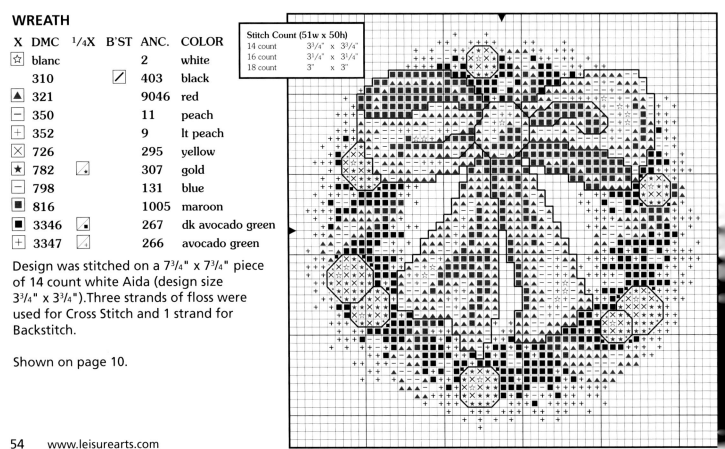

Stitch Count (41w x 37h)		
14 count	3"	x 2³/₄"
16 count	2³/₄"	x 2¹/₂"
18 count	2¹/₂"	x 2¹/₄"

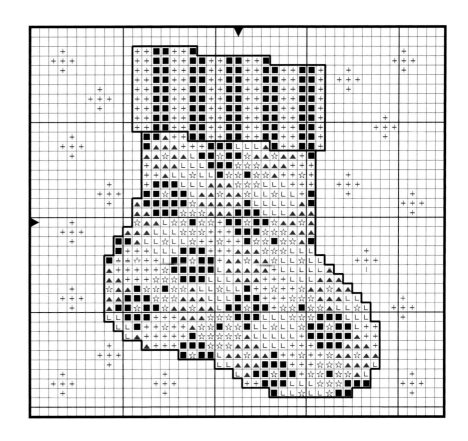

Design was stitched on an 7" x 7" piece of 14 count white Aida (design size 3" x 2³/₄"). Three strands of floss were used for Cross Stitch and 1 strand for Backstitch and French Knots.

Shown on page 15.

PATCHWORK STOCKING

X	DMC	B'ST	ANC.	COLOR
☆	blanc		2	white
▲	321		9046	red
■	700	╱	228	green
+	704		256	lime green
L	726		295	yellow

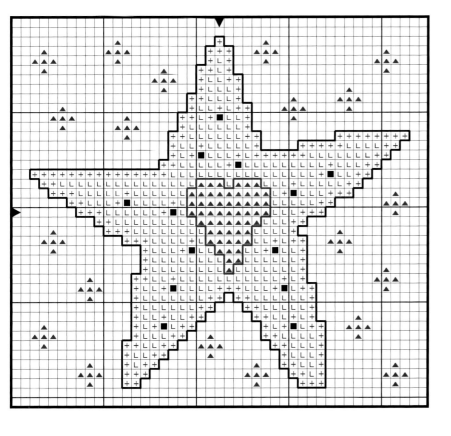

Stitch Count (41w x 37h)		
14 count	3"	x 2³/₄"
16 count	2³/₄"	x 2¹/₂"
18 count	2¹/₂"	x 2¹/₄"

Design was stitched on a 7" x 7" piece of 14 count white Aida (design size 3" x 2³/₄"). Three strands of floss were used for Cross Stitch and 1 strand for Backstitch.

Shown on page 15.

STAR

X	DMC	B'ST	ANC.	COLOR
▲	321	╱	2	red
■	700	╱	228	green
+	704		256	lime green
L	726		295	yellow

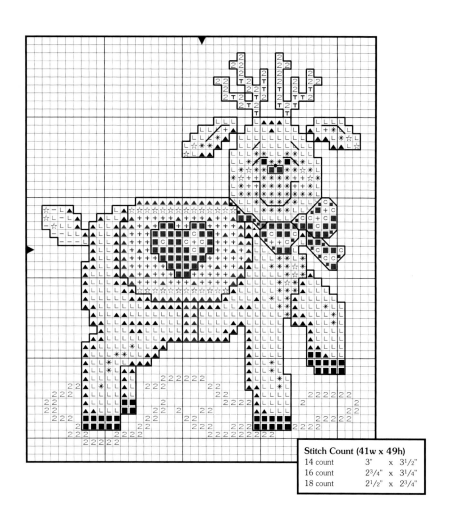

PRANCING REINDEER

X	DMC	1/4X	B'ST	ANC.	COLOR
☆	blanc			2	white
■	321	▪	╱	9046	red
C	351			10	dk peach
+	352			9	peach
▲	435	◢		1046	golden brown
L	437	◣		362	beige
▲	702			226	green
✳	739			387	beige
−	746			275	lt yellow
+	772			259	lt green
2	775			128	baby blue
T	809			130	blue
■	3371		╱	382	dk brown
☆	3820			306	gold
●	blanc			2	white Fr. Knot

Design was stitched on a 7" x 7½" piece of 14 count white Aida (design size 3" x 3½"). Three strands of floss were used for Cross Stitch and 1 strand for Backstitch and French Knots.

Shown on page 6.

Stitch Count (41w x 49h)

14 count	3"	x	3½"
16 count	2¾"	x	3¼"
18 count	2½"	x	2¾"

ROCKING HORSE

X	DMC	1/4X	B'ST	ANC.	COLOR
Z	321			9046	red
■	700			228	green
C	702			226	dk lime green
✕	726			295	dk yellow
✳	739	◢		387	beige
−	746			275	lt yellow
C	816		╱	1005	maroon
▲	920	◢		1004	rust
▲	922	◢		1003	lt rust
■	3371	▪	╱	382	dk brown

Design was stitched on a 8" x 7½" piece of 14 count white Aida (design size 4" x 3½"). Three strands of floss were used for Cross Stitchand 1 strand for Backstitch.

Shown on page 15.

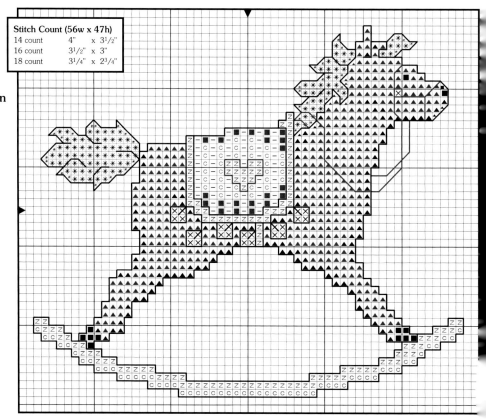

Stitch Count (56w x 47h)

14 count	4"	x	3½"
16 count	3½"	x	3"
18 count	3¼"	x	2¾"

BEAR

X	DMC	¼X	B'ST	ANC.	COLOR
☆	blanc			2	white
+	310	◢	◥	403	black
−	321	◢		9046	red
+	351			10	dk peach
▲	435			1046	golden brown
L	437	◢		362	lt golden brown
−	676			891	gold
■	702			226	dk lime green
▲	704			256	lt lime green
✕	726			295	dk yellow
S	727	◢		293	yellow
入	739	◢		387	beige
2	775	◢		128	baby blue
■	816	◢		1005	maroon

Design was stitched on a 7" x 7½" piece of 14 count white Aida (design size 3" x 3½"). Three strands of floss were used for Cross Stitch and 1 strand for Backstitch.

Shown on page 14.

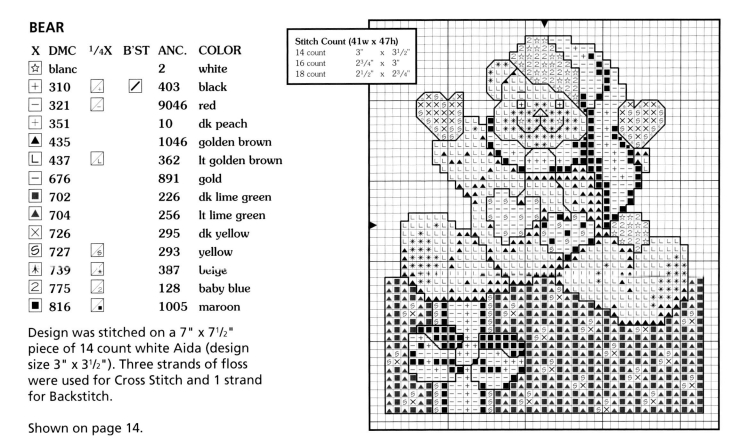

Stitch Count (41w x 47h)		
14 count	3"	x 3½"
16 count	2¾"	x 3"
18 count	2½"	x 2¾"

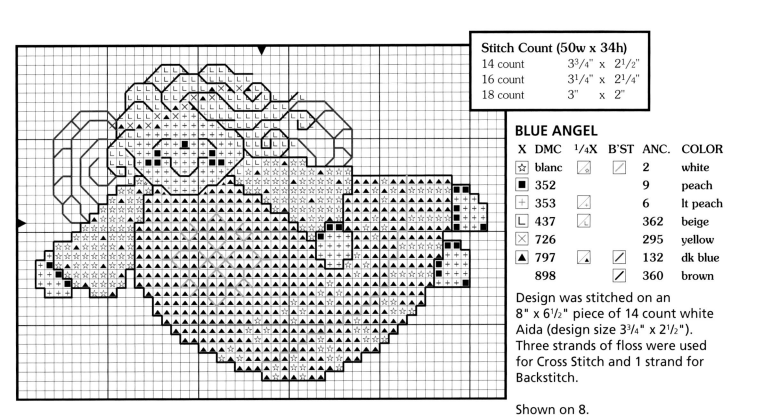

Stitch Count (50w x 34h)		
14 count	3¾"	x 2½"
16 count	3¼"	x 2¼"
18 count	3"	x 2"

BLUE ANGEL

X	DMC	¼X	B'ST	ANC.	COLOR
☆	blanc	◢	◥	2	white
■	352			9	peach
+	353	◢		6	lt peach
L	437	◢		362	beige
✕	726			295	yellow
▲	797	◢	◥	132	dk blue
	898		◥	360	brown

Design was stitched on an 8" x 6½" piece of 14 count white Aida (design size 3¾" x 2½"). Three strands of floss were used for Cross Stitch and 1 strand for Backstitch.

Shown on 8.

RED ANGEL

X	DMC	1/4X	B'ST	ANC.	COLOR
☆	blanc		╱	2	white
▲	321	◣	╱	9046	red
■	352			9	peach
+	353	◢		6	lt peach
L	437	◣		362	beige
☒	726			295	yellow
	898		╱	360	brown

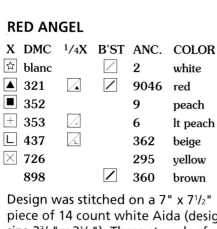

Design was stitched on a 7" x 7½" piece of 14 count white Aida (design size 2¾" x 3½"). Three strands of floss were used for Cross Stitch and 1 strand for Backstitch.

Shown on page 8.

Stitch Count (38w x 48h)		
14 count	2¾"	x 3½"
16 count	2½"	x 3"
18 count	2¼"	x 2¾"

NATIVITY ANGEL

X	DMC	1/4X	B'ST	ANC.	COLOR
☆	blanc	◢		2	white
C	164	◢			lt green
n	225	◢		1026	pink
■	321		╱	9046	red
▲	436	◣		1045	golden brown
▲	676	◣		891	gold
−	677	◢		886	lt gold
☒	726			295	dk yellow
+	727			293	yellow
+	754	◢		1012	peach
	801		╱	359	brown
−	948	◢		1011	lt peach
■	987		╱	244	dk green

Design was stitched on a 7" x 7¾" piece of 14 count white Aida (design size 3" x 3¾"). Three strands of floss were used for Cross Stitch and 1 strand for Backstitch.

Shown on page 7.

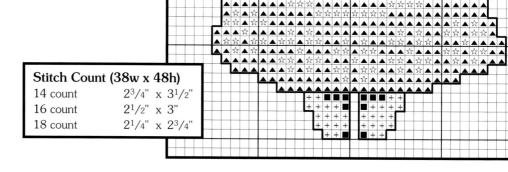

Stitch Count (40w x 50h)		
14 count	3"	x 3¾"
16 count	2½"	x 3¼"
18 count	2¼"	x 3"

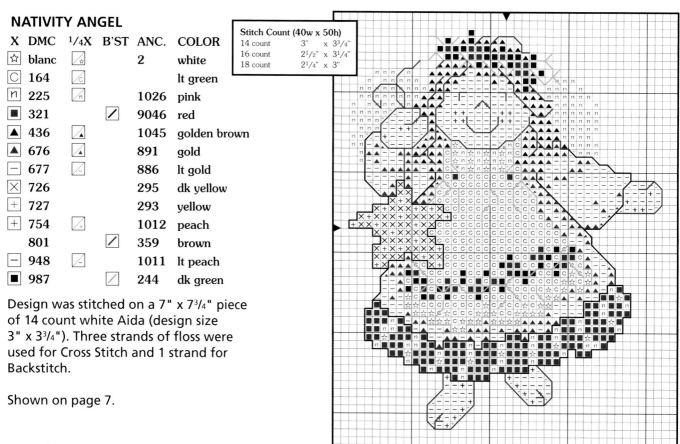

NATIVITY

X	DMC	1/4X	B'ST	ANC.	COLOR
☆	blanc			2	white
Z	321	z		9046	red
+	435	+		1046	dk golden brown
▲	676	▲		891	gold
L	677	L		886	lt gold
+	754			1012	peach
	796		/	133	dk blue
■	798	■		131	blue
n	800	n		144	vy lt blue
2	809	2		130	lt blue
	895		/	1044	vy dk green
■	898	■	/	360	dk brown
−	948	−		1011	lt peach
▲	987	▲		244	dk green
C	989	C		242	green
✳	3837			100	purple
●	898			360	dk brown Fr. Knot

Stitch Count (49w x 56h)		
14 count	3 1/2"	x 4"
16 count	3 1/4"	x 3 1/2"
18 count	2 3/4"	x 3 1/4"

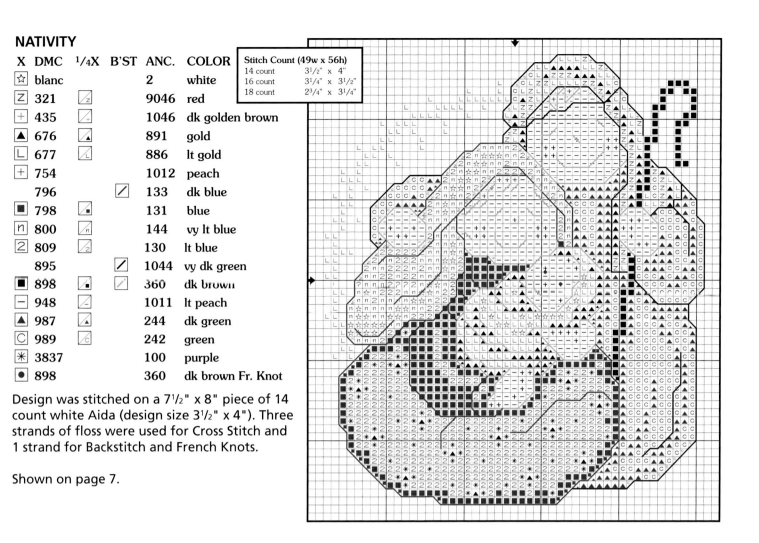

Design was stitched on a 7 1/2" x 8" piece of 14 count white Aida (design size 3 1/2" x 4"). Three strands of floss were used for Cross Stitch and 1 strand for Backstitch and French Knots.

Shown on page 7.

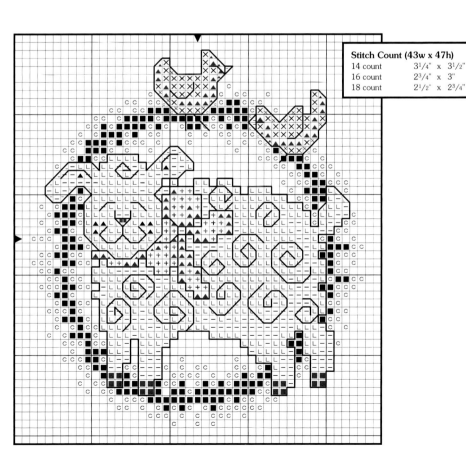

Stitch Count (43w x 47h)		
14 count	3 1/4"	x 3 1/2"
16 count	2 3/4"	x 3"
18 count	2 1/2"	x 2 3/4"

NATIVITY SHEEP

X	DMC	1/4X	B'ST	ANC.	COLOR
▲	321	▲		9046	red
+	351			10	dk apricot
+	352			9	apricot
✕	498	✕		1005	red
▲	754			1012	peach
−	842	−		1080	beige
■	898	■	/	360	dk brown
■	987			244	dk green
C	989	C		242	green
L	3866	L		926	off white

Design was stitched on a 7 1/4" x 7 1/2" piece of 14 count white Aida (design size 3 1/4" x 3 1/2"). Three strands of floss were used for Cross Stitch and 1 strand for Backstitch.

Shown on page 7.

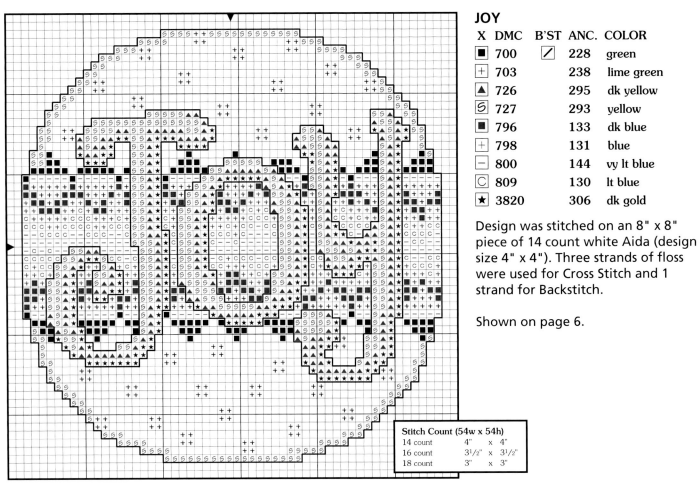

JOY

X	DMC	B'ST	ANC.	COLOR
■	700	/	228	green
+	703		238	lime green
▲	726		295	dk yellow
S	727		293	yellow
■	796		133	dk blue
+	798		131	blue
−	800		144	vy lt blue
C	809		130	lt blue
★	3820		306	dk gold

Design was stitched on an 8" x 8" piece of 14 count white Aida (design size 4" x 4"). Three strands of floss were used for Cross Stitch and 1 strand for Backstitch.

Shown on page 6.

Stitch Count (54w x 54h)

14 count	4"	x	4"
16 count	3½"	x	3½"
18 count	3"	x	3"

POLAR BEAR

X	DMC	¼X	B'ST	ANC.	COLOR
■	311	▪		148	blue
■	321			9046	red
	415		/	398	grey
+	726	▨	/	295	yellow
+	989			242	green

Design was stitched on an 8" x 8" piece of 14 count white Aida (design size 4" x 4"). Three strands of floss were used for Cross Stitch and 1 strand for Backstitch.

Shown on 7.

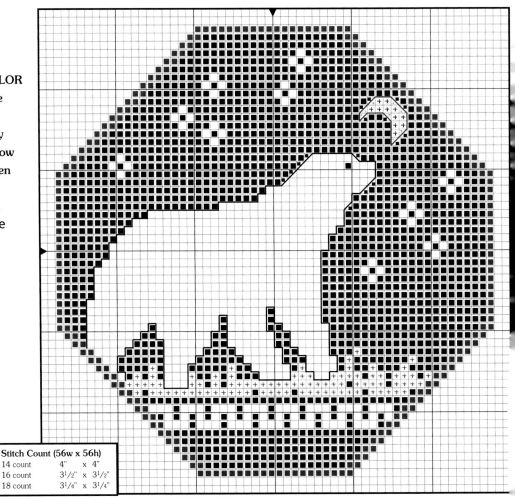

Stitch Count (56w x 56h)

14 count	4"	x	4"
16 count	3½"	x	3½"
18 count	3¼"	x	3¼"

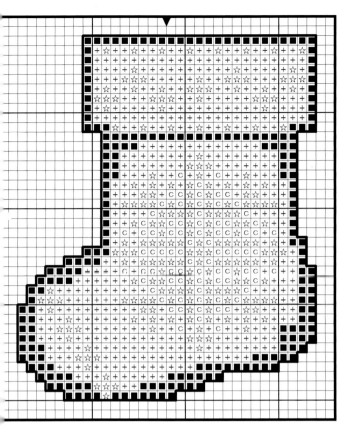

BLUE SNOWFLAKE STOCKING

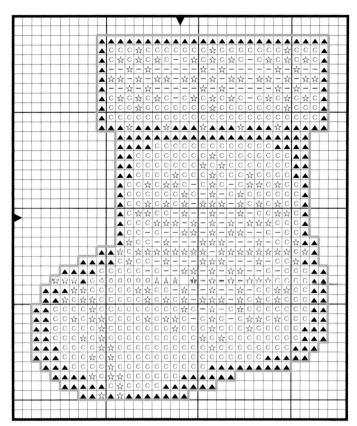

GREEN SNOWFLAKE STOCKING

Stitch Count (32w x 38h)

14 count	2¹/₂"	x	2³/₄"
16 count	2"	x	2¹/₂"
18 count	2"	x	2¹/₄"

SNOWFLAKE STOCKINGS

X	DMC	B'ST	ANC.	COLOR
☆	blanc		2	white
Z	321		9046	red
−	351		10	dk peach
▲	700	╱	228	lt green
C	702		226	lime green
−	704		256	lt lime green
■	796	╱	133	dk blue
+	798		131	blue
C	809		130	lt blue
▲	816	╱	1005	maroon

Each design was stitched on a 6¹/₂" x 7" piece of 14 count white Aida (design size 2¹/₂" x 2³/₄"). Three strands of floss were used for Cross Stitch and 1 strand for Backstitch.

Shown on pages 9, 10 and 15.

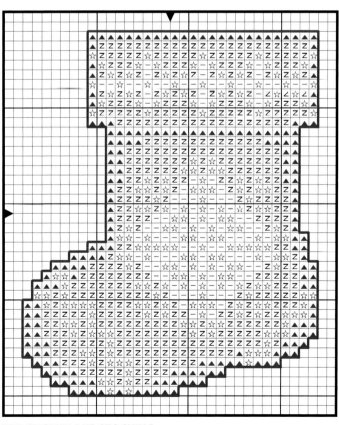

RED SNOWFLAKE STOCKING

POINSETTIA STOCKING

X	DMC	B'ST	ANC.	COLOR
■	321		9046	red
C	351		10	dk peach
+	352		9	peach
+	353		6	lt peach
−	677		886	lt gold
2	704		256	lt lime green
L	726		295	yellow
▲	816	╱	1005	maroon
■	895		1044	dk avocado green
▲	987		244	avocado green

Design was stitched on a 6½" x 7" piece of 14 count white Aida (design size 2½" x 2¾"). Three strands of floss were used for Cross Stitch and 1 strand for Backstitch.

Shown on page 10.

Stitch Count (32w x 38h)		
14 count	2½"	x 2¾"
16 count	2"	x 2½"
18 count	2"	x 2¼"

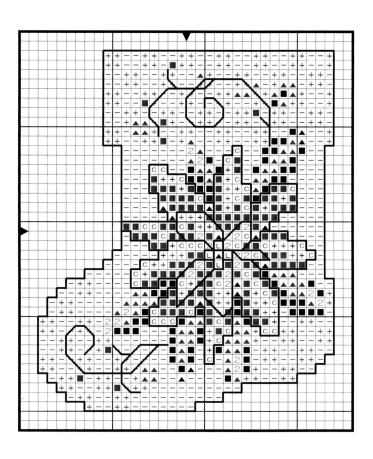

WREATH STOCKING

X	DMC	¼X	B'ST	ANC.	COLOR
■	321	◢		9046	red
C	351			10	dk peach
+	352			9	peach
−	712	╱		926	cream
L	726			295	yellow
+	739	◢		387	beige
▲	816	◢	╱	1005	maroon
■	986	◢		246	dk avocado green
▲	988	◢		243	lt avocado green

Design was stitched on a 6½" x 7" piece of 14 count white Aida (design size 2½" x 2¾"). Three strands of floss were used for Cross Stitch and 1 strand for Backstitch.

Shown on page 6.

Stitch Count (32w x 38h)		
14 count	2½"	x 2¾"
16 count	2"	x 2½"
18 count	2"	x 2¼"

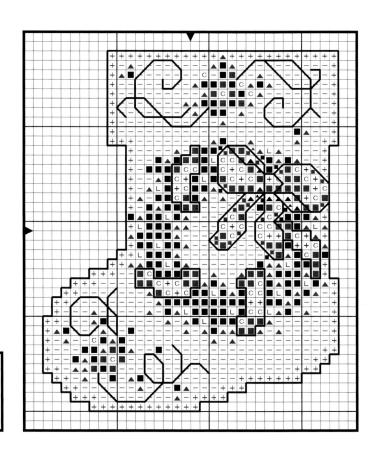

HOUSE

X	DMC	¼X	B'ST	ANC.	COLOR
☆	blanc	◹		2	white
■	321	◹		9046	red
+	352	◹		9	lt peach
■	435	◹		1046	golden brown
−	677			886	lt gold
	699		╱	923	dk green
C	703		◹	238	lt lime green
✕	726		◹	295	yellow
	816		╱	1005	maroon

Design was stitched on a 6½" x 7" piece of
14 count white Aida (design size 2½" x 3").
Three strands of floss were used for Cross
Stitch and 1 strand for Backstitch.

Shown on page 7.

Stitch Count (35w x 39h)		
14 count	2½"	x 3"
16 count	2¼"	x 2½"
18 count	2"	x 2¼"

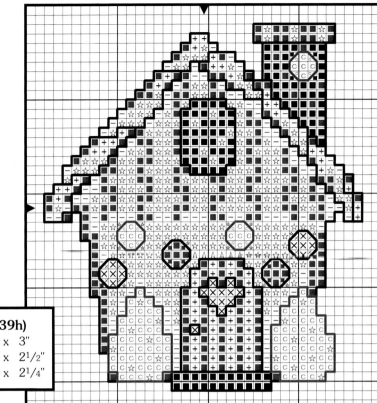

Stitch Count (36w x 45h)		
14 count	2¾"	x 3¼"
16 count	2¼"	x 3"
18 count	2"	x 2½"

SANTA HEAD

X	DMC	¼X	B'ST	ANC.	COLOR
☆	blanc	◹		2	white
Z	310		╱	403	black
▲	318			399	grey
Z	321			9046	red
C	351			10	dk peach
+	352	◹		9	peach
✳	420			374	golden brown
L	543			933	beige
C	676			891	gold
−	746			275	lt yellow
✳	762	◹		234	vy lt grey
■	816			1005	maroon
+	989			242	avocado green
	3852		╱	306	dk gold
▲	3864	◹		376	dk beige
●	blanc			2	white Fr. Knot

Design was stitched on a 7" x 7½" piece of 14 count
white Aida (design size 2¾" x 3¼"). Three strands of
floss were used for Cross Stitch and 1 strand for
Backstitch and French knots.

Shown on page 6.

TREE STOCKING

X	DMC	¼X	B'ST	ANC.	COLOR
■	321	◩	╱	9046	red
★	677	◩		886	lt gold
⌐	726			295	yellow
−	746	◩		275	lt yellow
	816		╱	1005	maroon
■	895	◩		1044	vy dk avocado green
✳	947			330	orange
▲	987	◩		244	avocado green
+	989			242	lt avocado green

Design was stitched on a 6½" x 7" piece of 14 count white Aida (design size 2½" x 2¾"). Three strands of floss were used for Cross Stitch and 1 strand for Backstitch.

Shown on page 10.

Stitch Count (32w x 38h)

14 count	2½"	x	2¾"
16 count	2"	x	2½"
18 count	2"	x	2¼"

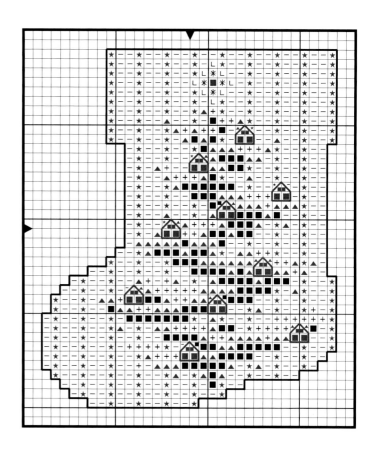

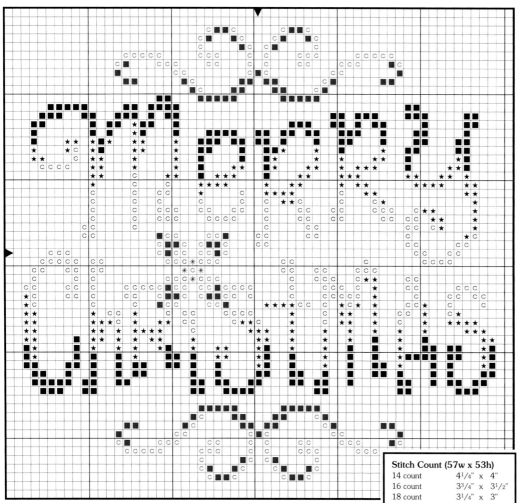

MERRY CHRISTMAS

X	DMC	ANC.	COLOR
◎	321	9046	red
■	700	228	green
★	702	226	lime green
◎	704	256	lt lime green
✳	726	295	yellow
■	816	1005	maroon

Design was stitched on an 8¼" x 8" piece of 14 count white Aida (design size 4¼" x 4"). Three strands of floss were used for Cross Stitch.

Shown on page 9.

Stitch Count (57w x 53h)

14 count	4¼"	x	4"
16 count	3¾"	x	3½"
18 count	3¼"	x	3"